Dennis Littky
with Samantha Grabelle

THE BIG PICTURE
Education Is Everyone's Business

Alexandria, Virginia USA

1703 N. Beauregard St. • Alexandria, VA 22311-1714 USA
Telephone: 800-933-2723 or 703-578-9600 • Fax: 703-575-5400
Web site: http://www.ascd.org • E-mail: member@ascd.org

Gene R. Carter, *Executive Director;* Nancy Modrak, *Director of Publishing;* Julie Houtz, *Director of Book Editing & Production;* Katie Martin, *Project Manager;* Reece Quiñones, *Senior Graphic Designer;* BMWW, *Typesetter;* Tracey A. Franklin, *Production Manager.*

Printed in the United States of America. Cover art copyright © 2004 by ASCD. Cover composition based on an original photo by Cally Robyn Wolk. Photo of John Dewey courtesy of the Special Collections Research Center, Morris Library, Southern Illinois University. Photo of Marian Wright Edelman, © Michael Collopy, courtesy of The Children's Defense Fund. Photo of Myles Horton courtesy of The Highlander Center. Photo of Albert Schweitzer courtesy of The Albert Schweitzer Fellowship.

Photo Credits: Cally Robyn Wolk (iii, v, xiii, xviii, 18, 42, 72, 94, 110, 134, 170, 182, 202, 217), Jose Sauret (152): © 2002 by The Big Picture Company, used with permission; Samantha Grabelle (209); John Forasté (229); Lauren Grabelle (230).

ASCD Member Book, No. FY05–1 (September 2004, PCR). ASCD Member Books mail to Premium (P), Comprehensive (C), Regular (R) members on this schedule: Jan., PC; Feb., P; Apr., PCR; May, P; July, PC; Aug., P; Sept., PCR; Nov., PC; Dec., P.

Paperback ISBN: 0-87120-971-3 • ASCD product #104438 • List Price: $26.95
($21.95 ASCD member price, direct from ASCD only)
e-books ($26.95): netLibrary ISBN 1-4166-0058-2 • ebrary ISBN 1-4166-0059-0 • Retail PDF ISBN 1-4166-0276-3

Library of Congress Cataloging-in-Publication Data

Littky, Dennis.
   The big picture : education is everyone's business / Dennis Littky with Samantha Grabelle.
     p. cm.
   Includes bibliographical references and index.
   ISBN 0-87120-971-3 (alk. paper)
   1. Education—Aims and objectives—United States. 2. Student-centered learning—United States. 3. Effective teaching—United States. 4. School environment—United States. I. Grabelle, Samantha, 1970– II. Title.

   LB14.7.L58 2004
   3708.973—dc22   2004009161

20 19 18 17 16   4 5 6 7 8 9 10 11 12

"I came to high school without any expectations."

In middle school, I was known as the troublemaker, and I was a frequent visitor at the principal's office. The challenge of high school seemed far from real. I lacked the motivation and confidence to get me places. Then a friend told me about a new high school described in the newspaper. I was nowhere near being an honor student and close to quitting school altogether, but I took a chance for once and sent in an application. It didn't occur to me then why I took that chance. Now, I guess I did it for myself. I must have figured that if I didn't, who would? It was a mature decision, and the right one.

Change has been a part of my life since the day I began at The Met. It was a major difference from being in middle school. For one thing, I was given attention—something I was not accustomed to getting in the regular public school system. For many years, I did not speak up in class because I was afraid the teachers would reject me. I was used to being shunned away like the problem kid.

Maybe because of this, during the first few weeks of school at The Met, I got into a number of conflicts with other students. The tribulations of my life were constant. There were many moments when I felt confused as to who I really was. I thought I would build a "tough girl" image because I did not want others to mess with me; it had worked in middle school! However, at The Met, my self-perception began to change. I kept journals throughout my four years there, and from time to time, I still read them. In one entry I reread recently, I saw this question, asked as if I would get a reply: "Why do these people at school care so much?"

I wonder now why I would ask such a silly question. The answer was shown to me every day at The Met. I had a family at school. The same students were in my advisory for the full four years. We built a close bond with each other and with our advisor, Charlie. (It would have been awkward to call him "Mr. Plant," like students do at traditional schools. It just wasn't The Met way.) All of us referred to our advisor by his first name, and our advisory was "Charlie's Angels." We would have dance sessions together, celebrate birthdays, do mock trials, and reflect on what we accomplished over the course of each week. It was a support network that couldn't be broken. I felt comfortable letting my advisory know about what bothered me or how I felt, and our relationships with each other grew throughout the years.

My family is amazed at how I am still involved with The Met. I am in college now, an alumna from the first graduating class, and even today, I get phone calls from Charlie, letters, care packages, and even access to my old school. I feel that I am always welcome there.

I sometimes wonder where I would be now without the support I got from my high school. I was fortunate enough to have people who believed in me. My attitude changed toward myself and toward others. At The Met, I learned that to make my learning real, I had to *do something*. And I did.

The Met gave me the opportunity to shine. The people there saw me as a kid with potential. In a traditional school setting, I would have been given low scores . . . or I might have even failed out. Truly, I think that The Met helped me develop the strength to persevere through the hardships I've faced in my life. It feels good to know that there, I mattered as a student and as an individual, and that the people cared too much about me to leave me behind.

Mareourn Yai

The Met, Class of 2000
Lesley University, Class of 2005

THE BIG PICTURE
Education Is Everyone's Business

Foreword

On Being Bold

by Deborah Meier

For a century or more, reformers have been fiddling with how to improve on a paradigm of schooling derived from another age and intended for a very different purpose. Thousands of years of history suggest that the schoolhouse as we know it is an absurd way to rear our young; it's contrary to everything we know about what it is to be a human being. For example, we know that doing and talking are what most successful people are very good at—that's where they truly show their stuff. We know that reading and writing are important, but also that these are things that only a rather small and specialized group of people is primarily good at doing. And yet we persist in a form of schooling that measures our children's "achievement" largely in the latter terms, not the former . . . and sometimes through written tests alone.

Dennis Littky has been gradually taking on the unmentionable. Suppose we just turned the whole thing upside down. Suppose we went back to the oldest and most traditional idea of education: Let kids learn in settings where adults are doing interesting work. Let novices learn from masters. Then create a part-time community for kids where they can use their expanding knowledge of the real world as the foundation for new growth—an environment where they can learn about being a member of a peer group, where they can reflect on what they are doing at their work sites, and where they can hone skills and explore concepts that, they are coming to realize, will be critical to their futures.

Some people have these kinds of dreams for education reform, or hear about such dreams, and then sigh and say, "Can't be done." Nearly 10 years ago, I gasped when Dennis told me what he was up to in Providence, Rhode Island. Around that time, I had taken a few bold steps in a similar direction at Central Park East Secondary School and found myself beating my head against a very tough wall, trying to make my model work for a whole set of kids who deserved a better fit for who they were and for what society needed of them. But I believed that Dennis could do what he planned to do. He had the talent, the courage, the smarts—and the energy—to offer the world an entirely different model. He took a few more bold steps, and in doing so, invented something that was wholly new but rooted in something wholly old. And it fits.

These days, it is customary for reformers to say things like, "This is our last chance." That's nonsense, of course. As long as there are kids, there will be more chances. But it sure is the right time and place for us to attend to what Dennis has accomplished, especially if we are in any way serious about ensuring that all children can learn to new and higher standards. I add the last phrase because it's critical. All kids are always learning; but *what* are they learning?

It's also critical that we extend our concept of "new and higher" beyond traditional 14th-century academic terms. Even the aristocratic elite didn't send all their sons into the clergy or into academia; yet most of the schools we have invented are built on the assumption that everyone should become either academic scholars or monks.

Dennis is an intellectual, but he is also a big kid who loves to play with ideas and satiate his curiosity about how old ideas can be put together in new ways that are more palatable to skeptical publics: parents, local school boards, legislators, and, always, kids. He is also a master kid-person, but one of those rare ones whose love of being with children is absolutely on par with the pleasure he gets from adult company and from his capacity to operate in almost every domain. He's a joy-monger: full of tricks, including tricks for turning something seemingly impossible into something down-to-earth possible.

For more than 30 years, he has led the way. Dennis started his career in the 1960s, as a community leader in Ocean Hill-Brownsville, an African American neighborhood in Brooklyn, where he trained parents to get involved in their local schools. Then he set up a model teacher-training program at Stony Brook University on Long Island, where he first met his longtime friend and co-thinker, Elliot Washor. At the age of 27, Dennis became the first principal of a new "model" middle school, Shoreham-Wading River on Long Island. With his leadership, Shoreham became a national "State of the Art School" and one of the subjects of the book *Successful Schools for Young Adolescents*[1] by Joan Lipsitz. Well-known psychologist Leonard Krasner once wrote of Shoreham that it "may well be the most innovative use of designed environment in a school setting since John Dewey's Lab School."[2]

After Shoreham, Dennis took to the woods of New Hampshire to think and tinker, and ended up becoming principal of his small town's ailing high school. In a few years, he turned both Thayer Junior/Senior High School and the town of Winchester around, and got ordinary rural kids excited about being educated in ways none of them had ever imagined. During Dennis's tenure, the dropout rate at Thayer fell from 20 percent to 1 percent. College matriculation skyrocketed from 10 percent to 55 percent. Despite these successes, a conservative contingent of the community disagreed with Dennis's innovative, unorthodox approach and tried to have him fired. With the majority of the community behind him, Dennis never wavered. In 1993, he was a National Principal of the Year finalist and was honored as the New Hampshire Principal of the Year for his remarkable achievements at Thayer and his dedication to the students he was serving. The whole story is told in Susan Kammeraad-Campbell's 1989 book *Doc,*[3] which was adapted into the 1992 NBC-TV movie *A Town Torn Apart.*

It was while Dennis was at Thayer that we became friends and supporters of each other's work. Both of our schools were among the earliest members of Ted Sizer's Coalition of Essential Schools. Together, Dennis, Ted, and I became a working team: Dennis in a rural school, me in an urban school, and Ted as the philosopher of the group. All three of us came together at Brown University's Annenberg Institute for Educational Reform in 1994, and we continue to challenge each other to this day. We talk incessantly about how to make the world more receptive to our vision of schooling and how to have a bigger influence on efforts to meet the needs of today's kids and schools.

After Dennis left Thayer in 1994, he spent some time as part of Annenberg's think tank. Before long, though, the lure to be back in the thick of things led him to his next adventure. He and Elliot Washor launched The Big Picture

Company, a nonprofit education design organization, to take their big ideas for education out into the world and prove how commonsensical those ideas really were.

But Dennis is a school man. When he heard of Rhode Island's plan for a new vocational education school, he and Elliot took it as a challenge, and they turned it into something entirely different from, but utterly consistent with, the best intentions behind voc. ed. In 1996, in Providence, Dennis and Elliot started the first of the six schools that compose The Metropolitan Regional Career and Technical Center ("The Met"). The schools are small, intimate, and without yearlong classes. Truly. There are plenty of adults, and there is lots of learning and a whole city to learn from, but otherwise, The Met isn't a school at all in the usual sense of the word. For starters, the teenagers who are enrolled there show up every day, eager and ready to get started on their work and learning. Many of them are kids whose past attendance records were poor and whose achievements—at least as we usually measure them—were minimal. But at The Met, they all learn, learn, work, and work. Moreover, virtually all of them graduate and, yes, go on to college. Ninety-eight percent apply to college; 98 percent of those who apply are accepted. Seventy-five percent of them are the first in their families to continue their education past high school.

More and more people are interested in what's going on at The Met; this far-out idea has become "in." But the question now is, can an approach that works in Providence, under the watchful eyes of Dennis and Elliot, flourish elsewhere, in other hands? Dennis thinks yes. And I've learned to take whatever he thinks very seriously. With the guidance of The Big Picture Company, Oakland, Sacramento, El Dorado (Calif.), San Diego, Detroit, Chicago, Denver, Indianapolis, and Federal Way (Wash.) have already launched Big Picture Schools—small, personalized, public high schools modeled after The Met's design that work in tandem with their students' communities.

A lot of people have invested a lot in Dennis's idea, including the Bill & Melinda Gates Foundation, which has put millions of dollars behind its faith that The Met approach can work all over the country. And I, too, have a big stake in believing he can do this elsewhere, because I have yet to see another educational approach that works as well for as many of the so-called "at-risks." The Met's design is infused with respect for the kinds of values—like rigorous work and citizenship—that we desperately need today. Dennis's own workaholic energy, his love for a job well done and never less than well done, is part of what it's all about. He's a dyed-in-the-wool practitioner, steeped in theory and making it up as he goes. It's intriguing that in 2002, monolithic textbook publisher McGraw-Hill awarded Dennis, the "learning is not about textbooks" champion, their prestigious Harold W. McGraw Jr. Prize in Education.

There isn't a part of the job that Dennis hasn't tackled, from running successful schools in suburban, rural, and urban settings to worrying about the bathrooms, the architecture, the food, the kids' families, his staff's morale, the climate in the state capitol, who's up to what downtown, and how to get the press to cover a good story. He does it all and thinks about it all. His long-time partnership with Elliot Washor is one of those great stories of a successful working alliance that gives them both a far wider outreach than either could have had alone. Take everything Dennis says here in this book as gospel truth and put it to good use. The important thing is not just this or that idea of his—it's the big picture, the whole ball of wax, or whatever expression you like best. He has hold of a Big Idea that can transform the lives of millions of children, and maybe transform the nation as well. Oh, I know, I'm sounding a bit overboard, but what Dennis is doing is part of the small core of important work being done in this nation that offers us real hope. So we need to take heed.

Deborah Meier has spent 40 years in urban public education and is currently the co-principal of Mission Hill, a K–12 public school in Boston. She is best known for her work in the Central Park East schools in Harlem and for her role in founding the Coalition of Essential Schools.

Preface

... So Doc, what whispered The Met into your ear and put fire behind it to make it spark? When did you know that you were going to do what you just did? See, you done started something, Doc. I hope that you don't think that we are all going to go back to being normal people. Especially after four years of an incredible education. I guess that you are waiting around, with your fingers crossed, to see what happens to all of us. I'll tell you. I know that the values and spirit behind "my school" will always be with me because they're in me. Yes, they're in me and I have to continue to do something with them. They'll guide me when I'm in college and then maybe I'll start my own Met somewhere. Who knows? Anything is possible. ...

Sincerely,
Misty Wilson
The Met, Class of 2000
Brown University, Class of 2005
Met alumni volunteer, poet, activist

I started this book with Mareourn's essay, and now I've included these words from Misty, because even when we are looking at "the big picture," we cannot ever forget that we must start with the students. The kids must and always come first. There is no other way.

This book is an answer to Misty's opening question and a response to the great friends and colleagues who have been pushing me to write a book for years: something that would simply and concretely explain my philosophy and practice in a way that would help others to understand what I know is possible in education. I go back every year to my underlines in John Dewey's *Experience and Education;* to Herb and Judy Kohl's *The Long Haul,* about Myles Horton and the Highlander School;[1] and to Tom Peters's many books on successful businesses and leaders.[2] They all recommit me to my own philosophy and remind me why I do what I do. This is what I hope this book will be for the next generation of educators.

Before now, I was always too busy *doing* schools to find the time to *write* about them. Still, I have been writing regularly for more than 30 years. In 1972, when I started my first school, I began a tradition that has lasted through two other schools, a nonprofit organization, and now an entire network of schools across the country. Every Friday, I distribute a "TGIF" memo, which contains some personal reflections, my upcoming schedule, and important announcements for the week to come. On the left, there's an example of the kind of stuff I write about.

In the first years of the TGIF memo, some teachers began including their own writing in it, and that became part of the tradition, too. I love the TGIF and the personalized sharing it promotes among staff. Listening to teachers talk about their work, or appreciate their kids,

TGIF May 4, 2001

. . . Visitors from Vermont were in this week, and it was a great experience showing them around. What a perspective--they were just blown away. The kids always seem to say the right thing. One student said he worked hard because the work was his. Freshmen talked about what it was like coming into such a respectful and welcoming community. And one visitor thought we'd set him up when he saw the quality of the work the student sitting next to him had done. Then the student mentioned he had failed in four high schools before coming here. . . .

or verbalize their struggles always moves me. I love reading our Met staff's words in the TGIF and often get choked up, on the verge of tears actually, when I see what they have to say.

In more than 30 years, I haven't missed writing in a single TGIF. Each Thursday night, I sit down, look back at my week, react, analyze, reflect, and plan. It's been my way to make myself take account of where I am and let my staff know where I will be. So, in a way, this book is the ultimate TGIF. (Don't worry, Met staff, I won't ask you to write one this long—at least not this week.)

When I first hired Samantha Grabelle as my assistant, she, too, started to question me about why I hadn't yet written my own book. I gave her all my regular excuses, but this time there was an obvious solution. Sam said she would read through everything I had ever written (all my articles and all my TGIFs) and everything that had ever been written about me, and meet with me for several hours each week to record me talking about my philosophy, my life, and all the many stories I love to tell. So we met, and talked, and wrote, and rewrote, and many months later, the book is ready to share.

Of course, this book is much bigger than Sam and me. It is a gathering of all the thoughts and feelings and doings in my life, which in turn were influenced by all the thoughts and feelings and doings of the people close to me. The stories are not all mine; as in any storytelling culture, they are a combination of events that I witnessed, that happened around me, or that were told to me. I hope I have done the tellers and the characters justice. I should note, though, that I have changed some of the characters' names and that I've changed all of the students' names, except in cases where I've quoted their writing and secured their permission to include it. I expect this book will be very familiar to my friends, colleagues, and students, and I hope it is inspiring to those who have been or are going to be part of the personalized, small-school, educational change movement.

When Elliot Washor and I set up The Met, we did so to provide an example of what school *could* be like. Most of our credibility has come from the success of The Met, but our cause, our goal, was and *is* much bigger. We want to kick off a movement of people wanting schools like The Met. At the most basic level, this means a movement that sees education as everyone's business and views schools as much more than just buildings where teachers teach and students learn. A movement that is passionate about educating one student at a time, about evaluating students with multiple forms of assessment, and about measuring students' progress against real-world standards. A movement that values students as individuals; values families as integral to each child's learning; values communities as resources; and values educators as change agents who, together, have the power to better our neighborhoods, cities, states, countries, and world.

This is not a book about how to start a Met school. It is a collection of ideas and stories meant to help people understand a certain way to do things—a way that has worked for many. I know that if a movement is to go forward, those who would advance it must build on the past rather than start over again and again. But the stories and ways of doing presented here are not just the past but the present, as well. We are doing all of it right now, here in Providence, Rhode Island, at The Met, and throughout the United States at our Big Picture Schools, which we have developed around The Met model. My hope is that this book can provide a jumping-off place—not just theory, but theory attached to a real school, to real people, and to the real world of right now. The model works. It is flexible and it is real and it is exactly what kids need. Don't just take my word for it, either. Eliot Levine did a great, detailed study of The Met in his book *One Kid at a Time*.[3] It is a must-read.

I also hope that principals and teachers will read this book together and get reenergized about why we educators do what we do. I hope teacher educators will use it to encourage future teachers to see both the big picture *and* each individual student. And I hope parents and anyone else who cares about kids will read this book and be inspired to fight for an education system that includes them and their voices, and that allows schools to be true assets to our kids, our families, and our communities.

I want each chapter of this book to make you think, confirm ideas you've already had, and help you look at education in some new and different ways. I encourage you to write your thoughts and reactions in the margins and underline or circle anything that jumps out at you. In addition, there are questions at the end of each chapter to help you think more deeply about the issues raised. If you work in a school, you might want to look at these questions and tweak the wording so they are relevant and helpful to your efforts to bring about change in your school. Share the questions with fellow staff members. Compare answers at staff meetings and learn where your efforts converge and diverge. You could even develop entire staff retreats around these questions.

If you are a teacher educator, you might use the questions to help your students develop their own education philosophies. Use them to guide on-site observations of schools, or to help your students to formulate plans of action once they have their own students.

If you are a high school student, parent, or community member, look for questions that might provoke discussion about the current state of your local schools and the possibilities for growth and change.

Finally, if you are someone who can affect or create policy, please look at the questions as prompts to influence your work in changing and improving our education system.

As Misty wrote in her letter, *anything is possible*.

"Education is not preparation for life;
education is life itself."

~ John Dewey

1

The Real Goals
of Education

When I watch kids walk into the building on their first day of school, I think
about what I want them to be like when they walk out on their last day. I
also think about what I want them to be like on the day I bump into them
in the supermarket 10 or 20 years later. Over the course of three decades
watching kids walk into my schools, I have decided that I want them to

* be lifelong learners
* be passionate
* be ready to take risks
* be able to problem-solve and think critically
* be able to look at things differently
* be able to work independently and with others
* be creative
* care and want to give back to their community
* persevere
* have integrity and self-respect
* have moral courage
* be able to use the world around them well
* speak well, write well, read well, and work well with numbers
* **truly enjoy their life and their work.**

To me, these are the real goals of education.

I want students to learn to use the resources around them. I want them to read something or see something they are interested in and follow up on it. I want them to have an idea and then get on the phone and call people they can talk to about it, or pick up a book and read more about it, or sit down and write about it. When I imagine one of my students as an adult, I imagine a person who is a thinker and a doer, and who follows his or her passions. I see an adult who is strong enough to stand up and speak for what he or she wants and believes, and who cares about himself or herself and the world. Someone who understands himself or herself and understands learning. Creativity, passion, courage, and perseverance are the personal qualities I want to see in my graduates. I want them to come upon things they've seen every day and look at them in a whole new way. I want them to feel good about themselves and be good, honest people in the way they live their lives. And, catchphrase or not, I want my students to score high on the "tests of emotional IQ" that life will inevitably throw at them over and over again.[1]

Finally, I want my students to get along with and respect others. Someone once asked me, "What is the most important thing a school does?" I replied that everything I believe about the real goals of education is not possible if the kids in the school do not care about and cannot get along with each other or with the people they meet outside of school. I believe that this is at the heart of what we mean when we talk about celebrating and respecting diversity, and it is at the heart of what makes a school and a society work.

When a kid leaves my school, I want her to have the basic life skills that will help her get along in the adult world—like knowing how to act in a meeting or how to keep her life and work organized. Basic stuff that too many schools forget about in their rush to cram in three sciences, three social studies, four maths, and so on. But I also want her to be the kind of person who will keep building on what she got in my school, who will keep developing skills, keep learning, keep growing. Each of us, if we live to be just 70 years old, spends only 9 percent of our lives in school. Considering that the other 91 percent is spent "out there," then **the only really substantial thing education can do is help us to become continuous, lifelong learners.** Learners who learn without textbooks and tests, without certified teachers and standardized curricula. Learners who love to learn. To me, this is the ultimate goal of education. W. B. Yeats said it this way: **"Education is not the filling of a pail but the lighting of a fire."**

———————◆———————

In 1999, the school board in Howard County, Maryland, removed two criteria from its official policy on determining high school students' grades. You know that neither of them were standardized tests. No, they were, and I quote, "originality" and "initiative." This school board decided that those two qualities of a student's work were no longer important. They decided this because, they said, it is "impossible" to measure how hard a student tries or if a student's work is original. What they were really saying, and what way too many school boards are now saying, is this: If it can't be measured *easily,* then we can't care about it, we can't teach it, and we certainly can't determine if a kid has learned it. The solution? Take originality and initiative completely out of your educational goals and just teach to the test. It makes me scream.

Ernest L. Boyer, the renowned education expert and then-president of the Carnegie Foundation for the Advancement of Teaching, once gave a speech entitled "Making the Connections." In it, he said (beautifully),

I know how idealistic it may sound, but it is my urgent hope that in the century ahead students in the nation's schools will be judged not by their performance on a single test, but by the quality of their lives. It's my hope that students in the classrooms of tomorrow will be encouraged to be creative, not conforming, and learn to cooperate rather than compete.[2]

Boyer said this in 1993. He died two years later, after a long battle with cancer. Boyer knew that schools were headed in the wrong direction and he made that clear by saying that his hope was "idealistic." It is so sad to me that if he were here today, he would not only see how idealistic this hope *still* is, but how far we have gone since then in the exact opposite direction.

I remember in the 8th grade, my science teacher had us do these posters that he put up all around the school. Though it wasn't exactly a test, it *was* a major project, and we all knew our grade depended on it. So there these posters were, hung all over the walls, and they were beautiful, and the teacher looked good to his boss and colleagues, and he probably felt pretty good about himself, too. I think this was the first time I realized how much of my education was total bull. I knew I hadn't learned anything about what was on those posters, including my own. And the teacher just hung them up. We barely talked about the posters, we made no connection with them to anything else, and he never went any deeper with the learning than that final project. My classmates and I had simply copied pictures and words out of the encyclopedia, and for that we not only passed the test of poster making, but were also assumed to have gained the predetermined "set of knowledge" for that quarter. Never mind that none of us had learned very much about science, let alone about initiative or originality. We did exactly what the "test" required us to do and nothing more—and so did the teacher.

Today, tests as meaningless as that test of poster making are determining the goals of education. Tests are dictating what we as a society hold valuable in our young people. **Our addiction to testing is blinding us to what we believe in our hearts are the important lessons our children should learn.**

If we worked backward, and thought first about the kind of adult we admire, we would not name characteristics that could be measured on a multiple-choice test. No single measurement or tool can get at what's really important in any area of learning. And the current push for one test that every kid has to pass in order to move to the next grade or graduate makes the whole situation even sadder.

> What we want to see is the child in pursuit of knowledge, and not knowledge in pursuit of the child.
>
> ~ George Bernard Shaw

With their focus on end results, too many schools and education policymakers forget how much the *process* influences how a kid takes in knowledge and then uses it. **Too many forget how intrinsic motivation and desire are to learning.** So much of our entire approach to education in the United States cheats kids out of the chance to become lifelong learners.

I want students to be able to find the information they need, to be able to go through the process of **finding learning.** And the key is that they are motivated to do it. I care more that a student is excited to go deeper in her exploration of the history of women in her native country than I do about that student's ability to answer every question on a standardized U.S. history test. I care way more about helping kids learn to apply knowledge than I do about presenting them with knowledge and finding out if they have memorized enough of the facts to spit them back at me. Most schools just give out the knowledge and then test it. They explain photosynthesis and then ask the kid to spit back photosynthesis. In between, no photosynthesis-like process happened inside that kid! He didn't take in that knowledge and then go to the library to find more books about photosynthesis, call a local greenhouse to go see how it works, or speak to a scientist who studies plants. And he certainly didn't grow at all in between receiving the knowledge and being tested on it. He took it in and spit it right back out—the information and himself, unchanged.

So What Is Learning?

How do we know if our kids are becoming lifelong learners? If they are learning *right now*? If they are becoming "educated people"? I give a lot of speeches around the United States to people who walk into the room thinking they know what it means to be an educated person. They're ready to learn from me about *how* to educate, but they feel pretty confident that they know *what* an educated person looks like. And then I show them that famous scene from the movie *My Cousin Vinny*. You know the one I'm talking about. Marisa Tomei is on the stand proving to the jury that it couldn't possibly have been the defendants' car that left the tire tracks found at the scene. She spews out all kinds of facts and theories and historical knowledge about cars to demonstrate her case. She generalizes, she pulls things together, she teaches what she knows to the courtroom. It's an awesome scene. And then I stop the tape and ask the audience if they would consider her to be "an educated person." If I see that there are still people who think, "Well, but she's a hairdresser, so she can't *really* be educated," I sometimes ask them, "If she had the same knowledge about and passion for cars, but was a doctor instead of a hairdresser, would we consider her educated then?" Of course we would.

Regardless of who you are, if you can get up and be passionate about something and tell others about what you know, then you are showing that you are educated about that topic. This is what an *exhibition*[3] is: It is kids getting up and talking passionately about a book they've read, a paper they've written, drawings they've made, or even what they know about auto mechanics. It is a way for students to have conversations about the things they have learned. Exhibitions are the best way to measure learning because they put the kids right in the midst of their learning, which makes a lot more sense than asking them to sit quietly for an hour and fill in test bubbles with a pencil. And because exhibitions are interactive, they propel the kids to want to learn more. That is what matters.

I remember one time when I was taking a group of 8th graders on a trip to Washington, D.C., by train. The conductor was really having fun talking with them and hearing about their plans for the trip. The kids told him about the research they had done and the decisions they had made together. Then the train conductor told them he wanted to find out how smart they were. So he started quizzing them on state capitals. It is so sad to me that after everything he had learned about them—their unique personalities and skills—and after seeing how passionate they were about learning, he still wanted to know if they were *really* "smart kids," and he, like so many, thought a memorization test was the way to determine that.

Another example that I use to show people what learning really is is a segment of a videotape on math and science learning called *A Private*

Universe.[4] The video was produced by the Harvard-Smithsonian Center for Astrophysics and shows all these quick interviews with Harvard students, faculty, and alumni on graduation day. Most of them look so "educated" in their caps and gowns and flowing academic robes. And then the interviewer asks them one of two questions: "What causes the seasons?" or "What causes the phases of the moon?"

Twenty-one of the 23 randomly selected Harvard folks give the wrong answer. What's more, their wrong answers reveal the same misconceptions about these things that the answers of grade schoolers do. Then the interviewees are asked to list all the science classes they've taken over the years, either at Harvard or in high school. When I show this video to audiences, I say, "Come on, they've taken every kind of science course possible and passed every one of them, and done this and that, but they can't apply it to something as basic as the change of seasons!?" Because of their Harvard diplomas, these grads are going to become some of the most powerful people in our world, but what kind of power is it when you can't apply the knowledge that the diploma stands for? Elliot Washor, my longtime friend and the cofounder of The Met and The Big Picture Company, points out that this says a lot about how too many schools view learning. He relates it to what we are doing at The Met and our Big Picture schools in this way: "**They say knowledge is power. We say the *use of knowledge* is power.**"

My point is that learning is about going beyond the knowledge given to you in a class or in a book or at a museum. **Learning is personal.** It happens one on one, it happens in small groups, it happens alone. Sure, a conference, a speaker, a lecture is motivating—but the real learning happens after. It's what you do with it, how you integrate it, how you talk to your family, friends, and classmates about it. That's what learning is. As noted psychology and education expert Seymour Sarason reminded me recently, it's similar to psychotherapists' belief that patients don't get better *during* the hour, but *between* the hours.

I'm not suggesting we throw out everything schools do now or everything those Harvard kids learned. I'm suggesting that we look more deeply at what we define as learning and be honest and try different things and see what works. **Learning is about learning how to think.**

My new friend Tom Magliozzi, from National Public Radio's popular show *Car Talk,* has a lot to say about what learning really is in the book he and his brother wrote, *In Our Humble Opinion.* One of my favorite parts is when Tom, a man with a Ph.D. in chemical engineering from MIT, says this:

> It seems to me that schools primarily teach kids how to take tests (a skill one hardly uses in real life unless one is a contestant on a quiz show). Elementary school prepares kids for junior high; junior high prepares them for high school. So, the goal—if we can call it that—of schools is to prepare kids for more school.[5]

Psychologist Robert J. Sternberg has written about the dichotomy between his "real world" success and the difficulty he had studying psychology in college. Here's a quote from him that reminds us that, even in higher education, there is often a huge split between what we are taught and expected to learn, and what is actually important "out there":

> I have now been a psychologist for 21 years, and one thing of which I am certain is that I have never—not even once—had to do in the profession what I needed to do to get an *A* in the introductory course, as well as in some of the

other courses. In particular, I've never had to memorize a book or lecture. If I can't remember something, I just look it up. The way schools set things up, however, they reward with *A*s the students who are good memorizers, not just at the college level but at many other levels as well.[6]

Learning is not about memorizing. Learning is about being mindful. Mindfulness is a concept I learned about a while back, and it really makes sense to me as something we are trying to develop in our students at The Met. Ellen Langer is a professor of psychology at Harvard and the author of the books *Mindfulness*[7] and *The Power of Mindful Learning*.[8] In these books, she talks about how cultivating mindfulness is helping people realize that the world is full of interesting possibilities for learning, and that the world will always look different from different perspectives. **Our education system should see creating mindful learners as its goal.** Learners who are mindful of all that surrounds them and all that is inside them. Here's Langer, quoted in *Parade* magazine:

> Too often, we teach people things like, "There's a right way and a wrong way to do everything, regardless of the circumstances." What we should be teaching them is how to think flexibly, to be mindful of all the different possibilities of every situation and not close themselves off from information that could help them.
>
> I love tennis. When I was younger, I went to a tennis camp, and they taught me how to hold a racket when I served. Years later, I was watching the U.S. Open, and I realized that not one of the players held the racket that way.
>
> The problem comes in the way we learn. We are rarely taught conditionally: "This might be a good grip for you." Usually, we're taught: "This is the right grip." Being mindful—using imagination and creativity to learn what works best for you—is what makes the difference between an average player and a champ.[9]

Then What Is Teaching?

Teaching is Listening, Learning is Talking.

~ *Message painted on a Met advisor's truck by his students*

When I lay out my vision of the real goals of education in an orderly looking list, like I did on page 1, I worry about what people, teachers in particular, will do with it. I worry about what they will interpret it to mean about teaching. I don't believe that you can separate teaching from learning. Please don't look at my list and say, "OK, I agree that these are the things kids should learn, so now let's set out a rigid point-by-point curriculum that can be taught to a class of 25 students." To me, **the *act of being a teacher* is understanding these goals of education, understanding how learning works, and figuring out how to apply all this to each student, one at a time.** I know that it would be pretty easy for someone to take the goals I believe in and contort them so they fit nicely and easily into a lecture-based curriculum designed to be assessed with a standardized, multiple-choice test. But being a teacher—and building a system of education, for that matter—is about taking these goals and creating the best possible environment for supporting kids and learning. It is not about taking these goals and finding a way to fit them into the traditional methods of schooling.

Here's an example of how educators can miss the point: There are people who believe that learning to be a moral human being is the most important goal of education. So all these curricula have been developed around teaching moral character. There are textbooks with "moral conflict scenarios" that sound good on paper, but may have nothing to do with where a particular kid is at right now. Then there are multiple-choice tests to assess whether the kid knows what is moral and what is not. Morality is this huge, hands-on, real-world issue, and well-intentioned schools are taking the students' hands and world right out of the equation.

Just having the right goals is not the answer. It is how you reach those goals—*the act of teaching*—that is so critical. Another example: If we say that every student in the United States should understand democracy, which I think we all agree on, most people think, "OK, well, kids learn about democracy by reading the Constitution and talking about how it was developed, and so on." Yes, this is very cool stuff to know. But while they're learning these things, **most kids are not making one democracy-inspired decision throughout their entire 12 years of schooling.** Most kids either aren't allowed to or don't believe they have the right to make decisions about anything significant during the years they are in school. So, to me, if we're trying to teach kids about the importance of democracy and being good citizens and about voting and all that comes with it, we really should be giving kids the opportunities to make real decisions and take real responsibility for what is going on around them. They should actually *be* voting, not just talking about it.

The act of being a teacher is the act of taking the goals I've described and then using your skills and **love for kids** to figure out how to create the best environment to help your students reach those goals. At the same time, you have to remember that every kid approaches learning in an individual way and will meet those goals in that individual way. And every kid is coming to you with his own personal baggage that may have to be worked through before he can even begin to learn what you are trying to teach him. The teacher's role is to find what that way is for each kid. Teaching becomes figuring out how to see and listen to each kid, **one kid at a time,** so that the kid can reach the goals for himself or herself. It is about finding the right relationship between the student and the adult, the relationship that works well for both of them. And, most importantly, **teaching cannot happen in a vacuum.** The community and the child's family must be included in every way possible. Parents are the student's first and most important teachers and they cannot, and must not, be left out of the education equation—not even when there are "professionals" around.

———◆———

In the early 1970s, I was placing student teachers in schools with "open classrooms." These schools were influenced by a big movement in the '60s that said having kids doing projects in small groups was a better set-up for learning than the traditional lecture format. One of my student teachers, a young, idealistic woman, turned to me one day and said, "This is great, Dennis, but when am I really going to learn how to *teach*?" She was standing there in an exciting, rich learning environment, but she couldn't see it because it didn't match her idea of what teaching was, which was standing up in front of the room, looking out at quiet rows of faces, and pouring knowledge into them.

Teaching is so much more than I ever thought it would be.

~ *A Met advisor, after his first year*

Unfortunately, to most people, teaching is the giving of knowledge. What are you going to tell the students? What is your expertise? But teaching is really about **bringing out what's already inside people.**

At The Met, we have completely redefined teaching. We've even changed the name from "teacher" to "advisor" to symbolize how we're breaking the stereotypes surrounding the profession. Our teachers are not simply givers of knowledge, but adults who inspire the students to find their own passions and their own ways of learning and who provide support along the way. Not by being a charismatic lecturer, but by being a great coach, role model, motivator, advisor, and, yes, *teacher*. Not by showing students where to find the knowledge in the textbook, but by helping them find the knowledge in the real world. Not by giving kids the answers, but by brainstorming with them about how to solve the problems. Not by telling students what they have to read, but by letting them choose their own books, based on what they are interested in. Not by getting students to write papers that meet a certain set of classroom, school, or state standards, but by working with them one-on-one to revise their papers until they feel good about what they've written and it meets their *own* standards. At The Met, advisors are an integral part of **an environment that allows students the freedom to find themselves with the support and motivation of inspiring adults.** This, to me, is exactly what a school should be.

When we hire teachers at The Met, we do it in this really democratic way, with all of the staff and some students involved in the decision making. Our main criteria for new teachers are that they love and are committed to kids, and that they themselves are lifelong learners. When I am interviewing someone, I ask myself, **is this a person who can be a role model to a kid through his or her own excitement about learning?**

I also try to see how they interact with kids. Are they relating to them and respecting them? If I get a chance to observe candidates in a teaching context, I am more interested in where their attention is than I am in how good the lesson is: Are they more interested in the content or the sound of their own voice than they are in the kids sitting right in front of them?

> We have plenty of people who can teach what they know, but very few who can teach their own capacity to learn.
>
> ~ *Joseph Hart*[10]

When a teacher loves kids, is excited about the act of teaching, and is a learner himself or herself, *that* is when the best teaching happens—whether it is in his or her "area of expertise" or not. I once had a teacher who taught a class on the Bible, not as a religious work but as a piece of literature, and she had never really studied it before. She told me later that, during that class, she was the best teacher she had ever been, because she was on the same level with her students—she was experiencing it all for the first time right along with them. This meant she wasn't saying things like, "Look at the metaphors in here and compare them," but was actually asking questions that she herself didn't know the answers to, like, "What do we think about this passage compared to this one?" It was very exciting for her and very invigorating for her students.

Another time, I had a home economics teacher who had to teach math to a small group of students who were struggling. She herself was not very good at math. Some might say, "Oh, no, that will never work," but it was some of her most brilliant teaching. I would watch her sitting with those six girls, and they'd be figuring out those problems *together*. She was comfortable with the students knowing that she didn't know everything. She was comfortable with the idea that she was not just there as question answerer, but as a role model who could show kids how to *find* the answers. She wasn't yelling at them about why didn't they understand it; she didn't get impatient with their lack of knowledge. She really went through the learning experience *with* them. And they went through it with her.

This is not to say that teachers shouldn't know content. The more knowledge you have, the easier it can be to learn more because you know which questions to ask. But I believe that knowledge can also get in the way sometimes. It's terrific for teachers to have depth in a certain area, as long as they don't just hand it over. They have to use that deep understanding to help their students discover the learning on their own. **Teaching and learning are about problem solving. Education is the process by which you put teachers and learners in the best possible environment for them to do this together.** And the best possible environment is one where people feel safe, supported, and respected, and where kids *and* adults are excited and passionate about learning.

Questions to Further This Conversation . . .

1. What are *your* "real goals of education"?

2. How would you define the differences between "learning" and "knowledge"?

3. What is your reaction to Dewey's statement that "education is not preparation for life; education is life itself"?

4. Do you agree that "learning is personal"? If so, how would you go about explaining the concept to someone who may not be as convinced?

5. How do you learn best? How would you go about teaching your "own capacity to learn"?

6. What do *you* look like and feel like when you are really learning?

"I want to go to a good high school because it will keep me motivated to finish school. I really want a good future. The reason for this is because I don't want to go through what my mother did. I'm learning from her mistakes. She struggled through her whole life and I don't want to go through what she did."

~ From an 8th grader's application to The Met

"Please help my son have a better future."

~ From a parent's essay in her 8th grader's application to The Met

2

Kids, Schools, and the Bigger Picture

I don't need to repeat all of the terrible and scary statistics about our children in the United States—their dropout rates, their pregnancy rates, their depression rates, their suicide rates, their murder rates. OK, I'll give you a few that really break my heart. According to a study of the graduating class of 2001 conducted by the Manhattan Institute for Policy Research, a nonprofit, nonpartisan think tank, one out of every three U.S. students who enrolls in high school drops out before graduation.[1] One out of every three! For black, Native American, and Latino students the statistics are even scarier, with nearly one out of every two students dropping out. The Centers for Disease Control and Prevention reported in 2002 that suicide was the third leading cause of death among young people 15 to 24 years of age, and that from 1952 to 1995, the incidence of suicide among adolescents and young adults nearly tripled.[2] Sixteen percent of violent crime arrests in 2000 were of children under the age of 18.[3]

It is clear from the research (and from our own hearts) that there is a relationship between dropping out of school and poverty, and between a history of violence and acts of violence. Neglect plays a role in all of these problems, and, to me, one of the biggest perpetrators of neglect is the school system. **Our kids are dying, and we don't even know who they are.** So many of them don't think school, or adults in general, have anything to offer them. Too often they are right.

After more than 35 years in education, I continue to be angry and amazed at what goes on in our public school system. I am angry that we mistreat and disrespect our youth, especially our poor youth, most especially our poor youth of color. I am angry and amazed that more people don't see what I see. I really believe that kids' lives depend upon more adults understanding, and changing, what is really going on in our schools.

Kids

Those of us involved in kids' lives need to remember how fragile they are, especially teenagers. Even the toughest ones need us more than they would ever admit. As adults, we have the power to break their spirits with even the smallest word or gesture, and with some kids, we may never get a chance to help build them back up again.

Whenever I meet kids who have dropped out of school (which, sadly, is often), I talk with them and try to find out why they did it. Although I am sure that many factors figure in each kid's decision to quit school, a lot of the time what the kid sees as the main reason is something that seems really small: "Mr. Williams pissed me off"; "Mrs. H. just didn't treat me right"; "The principal kept giving me dirty looks." **Kids are so fragile.**

Today, they are also up against serious stuff that makes life incredibly hard even without the pressure of school. At The Met, one of our graduation requirements is to write a 75-page autobiography. (I wish I could publish them all; they are some of the most fabulous papers you will ever see coming out of a high school.) Lots of graduates have told me that the assignment was incredibly difficult, not because of the length, but because of how much they dreaded having to relive the pain they've felt in their lives. **You cannot look away from what kids really need.**

> I wish they all came in ready, eager and excited—but that's not the reality.
>
> *~ A Met advisor to potential teachers*

I have seen kids walk into my schools throwing up from morning sickness, or coming in every day from a different foster home after being abused by their parents. We had a student at The Met get in one morning, grab an adult he trusted, and tell the story of how, an hour ago, he had pulled a gun on his father to stop him from beating his mother. Another student walked in and handed his teacher a crack pipe, like the ones he'd been using since he was 9 years old. He had been about to use it again that day, but thankfully, he came to school instead.

There are kids in every city and town facing these same obstacles. The difference at The Met is that the students feel comfortable there and see the school as part of the solution rather than one of their many problems. The Met is small, personalized, and flexible enough to support them as people while they continue to learn as students. We understand that in order for a school to help a kid learn and succeed, the kid must be known. And **you cannot know a kid whose voice you don't listen to, whose interests are a mystery, whose family is excluded, and whose feelings are viewed as irrelevant to the educational process.** When even one teacher builds a strong relationship with a kid and his or her family, the school can become the place the kid runs to when things fall apart, rather than the place the kid drops out of, or—terrifyingly—discharges bullets into.

Even kids who aren't facing the tougher issues like neglect, abuse, or drug addiction still have needs that our current education system cannot meet. Kids need variety, they need to be heard, they need to feel good about themselves. School structures must be sensitive to the tremendous physical, emotional, and intellectual upheaval brought on by adolescence alone. **Students need to feel that school is a safe place**—a place where they won't be punished indiscriminately, where the rules are clearly stated, and where the consequences of violating the rules are clear, too. They need to feel that school is a place where their strengths and energies are nurtured and applauded, where they and their loved ones matter as human beings, and where they have control of themselves and their successes. Finally, they need their school—and their society— to see them as a resource and not as a resource drain.

I believe what is wrong with education has a lot more to do with adults than with "the kids of today." One of the biggest problems with adults is their too-often low opinions and low expectations of kids. **While I think kids are very fragile, I also think they are very resilient** and can handle a lot more responsibility, challenge, and respect than adults give them credit for. Sometimes when I hear about a student's home life, I am amazed that he or she is able to function at all, let alone accomplish some of the amazing things I've seen. I think I get along so well with kids because I have incredible respect for them. I believe that every kid's got a certain beauty. My work as an educator has always been most fulfilling and exciting when I am part of a place that recognizes and supports the fragility in each kid, while it pushes every kid equally hard to reach his or her true potential.

Kids are also very attuned to adults' attitudes toward them. They can tell when you have low expectations for them, and it can hurt them pretty badly. For example, when Martha went to her guidance counselor at the beginning of 8th grade to start planning her high school career, the counselor told her flat out that she should not make plans to go to college because she would never get into one. Right then, Martha stopped functioning as a student. Although she knew that the counselor's statement was colored by racism, he succeeded in making her see no future for herself and no reason to put any more effort into school. I know that if not for The Met (or a school like it) welcoming Martha and expecting her to succeed and go on to college, she would have been lost—to the streets, to drugs or violence, or simply to a life where she continued to feel bad about herself. I'm boasting a little about The Met here, but I am so glad that Martha and so many students like her were offered, and grasped, the opportunity to come to a school like ours. The Met staff and I have always believed that we are in the business of saving children.

I have also always believed that it is of the utmost importance to give kids choices. As Max De Pree, a noted voice in organizational innovation, said so eloquently in his book *Leading Without Power:*

> To be without choices is a great tragedy, a tragedy leading to hopelessness or cynicism. . . . Without hope, it's difficult to explain existence and impossible to imagine a future. How, without hope, can you explain school to a child or the entailments of teenage pregnancy to a young woman?[4]

In the Preface, I mentioned that ever since my first job as a principal, I have been writing a weekly reflection in the TGIF, a memo that has evolved into a joint project of all the school staff. When I read the application essays of The Met's very first group of 8th grade applicants, this is what I wrote in that week's TGIF:

TGIF August 16, 1996

. . . Reading the most recent student applications brings tears to my eyes and anger to my heart. Thirteen-year-old students brilliantly articulating their wish to be educated, to learn. Bright students failing over and over again because, as they say, "no one cares." It is sad. It is revolting for our rich country to abandon our kids. There is no more important work than what we are doing. . . .

Most of our students at The Met, like most students everywhere, are ready to take responsibility for their own learning, are eager to be treated with respect, and have a lot to say about what *they* think should be the real goals of education. Although we are a public school and accept students by lottery, we require all applicants and their parents to write essays that explain to us why The Met is the right school for them. On the next two pages, you'll see excerpts from real 8th graders' application essays for the 2002–03 school year. I selected so many because they vary so much in content and because each one could easily be the words of thousands of children. I believe they represent the range of things most kids would say about education, if only education cared enough to listen. If the writing or grammar or depth of expression sound a little too good to be true, it is because these kids were writing about something that was important to them. This was not a meaningless exercise in "describing your dreams for your own education"; it was real, and these kids knew it.

. . . I think The Met would be great for me because I work better in small groups. The Met would be right for me. I will have a better learning environment to be in. I also work better if I have projects and lots of hands-on work to do.

. . . To tell you the truth I've made mistakes in my life (everyone does). I've gotten suspended three times. Also I am not doing good this year, but I want to become something one day. I hope that doesn't really change your feelings about choosing me.

. . . I would like to go to The Met school like my sister. She gets up at 5 every morning for school and she does not mind. I would like to like a school that much.

. . . I would like to attend The Met school because at the school I attend now . . . I feel like I have no room to succeed because the work and homework they give me is too easy so I tend to finish it in class. At your school I will be able to explore my limits through your internships. . . . I am worried that if I attend the [other] public high school, I'll get lost in the shuffle and forget my hopes and dreams.

. . . I would like to attend this school because I hear that a lot of people that have gone to The Met are in good universities . . . and I would like to go to one of those universities. The Met seems like a good school to get a good education for life.

... The reason why I would like to attend The Met is because it's a small school. I would be able to concentrate a lot more better. The teachers would be able to help more and explain more to you. It would also give the teachers a chance to figure out our strengths and weaknesses. I would be able to get a lot more help.

... The Met looks like a school that keeps their eye on all the students, not just the smart ones. I have friends that have gone to The Met and say it's a good school. I believe them because they are in college now.

... The opportunity to attend The Met would mean an open door, or option, for a change in my destiny. It would mean personal responsibility at an age where it is much required, and it would mean control of the way I learn, an option I have wanted to grasp since early in my life.

... I would like to attend The Met. I would also like the freedom that we don't experience in regular public schools. I also read that there are 14 students to 1 teacher. At my school it feels like we're lost in classrooms.

... I want to go to The Met because it is the only school where I will be able to express myself.

From the media, we hear these great, tearjerker stories of kids who succeeded despite the odds. But **all of our kids are facing the odds of an education system that is all wrong.** The odds are against them because the system works against them instead of with them. If we could start by simply paying attention to who kids are and where they are coming from, and then rebuild the system of education around that, we would immeasurably improve the odds that all our kids will succeed.

I see it every day: kids who have been dismissed as "dumb in math" or "uninterested in science" or "nonreaders" doing incredible things in these exact same areas because they were (finally) allowed to start with something they were already interested in. A 9th grade kid who "hates science" sees a movie about freezing people, then decides to read a college biology text on cryogenics, and then gives a presentation on it that would blow your socks off. A kid who has never been serious about anything to do with school starts staying after every day because she's so wrapped up in a project *she chose to do* on nonviolence and the civil rights movement. The rock-and-roll kid who's interning at a music store and learning how to calculate profits walks up in front of his peers and gives a 45-minute math demonstration. The quiet kid who loves computers but could never get any time on them at his old, crowded school gets an internship with a computer company and finds himself treated like a partner and valued for his knowledge and passion. I could go on and on.

Schools

I hate the idea that we put a box, "high school," around our discussion of adolescents. It's like we immediately stop thinking about the child and start thinking about things like seat time, test scores, class schedules, grade books, textbooks, special ed., gifted and talented programs, and so on. **We need to stay focused on the student,** whether that student is gifted and talented, special ed., or both (as most kids are).

Seymour Sarason talks in many of his books about how teacher education programs fail to train teachers to see and value the whole student. He compares this problem to that of medical education programs that prepare doctors to treat symptoms but not people.

Someone once said that **if we care about kids more than we care about schools, then we must change schools.** If you really just thought about the students, and not about "schooling," what kind of structures would you set up? If we all focused more on what we know about learning, rather than the "best way" to teach, what would education look like?

Think about **how people learn best.** We learn best when we care about what we are doing, when we have choices. We learn best when the work has meaning to us, when it matters. We learn best when we are using our hands and minds. We learn best when the work we are doing is—real and relevant.

We want to prepare our children for the world, so let's not isolate them from the world. Would you take a kid who's been standing in front of a hoop practicing free throws by himself for a year and then put him on a basketball court and expect him to know how to play the game? No! Of course not. But this is how schools are preparing kids for the real world.

Many people talk about how difficult it is to implement an integrated curriculum, which is taking the standard subject areas and combining them. That is ridiculous. The *world* is integrated! What is difficult is what schools do every day: unravel the world and all its vast knowledge and **put it into boxes called subjects and separate things that are not**

separate in the real world. What is science without math? What is history without language? What are languages without their history? I first started messing with the 45-minute periods schedule in the early '70s. I knew then that I was fighting a century-old addiction to teaching kids about the real world by locking them up in a building that looks, acts, and feels nothing like the real world. When we talk about reform, we should not be talking about tweaking the scheduling and modifying the curriculum, but about **completely overhauling the entire structure of schools** as we have known them for way too long.

> No matter how far you have gone on a wrong road, turn back.
>
> ~ *Turkish proverb*

Do most people even know how we got into this mess? In 1892, the National Education Association's (NEA) National Council formed the "Committee of 10." The president of Harvard University was the chair, and the other nine members were equally intellectual types from the elite institutions of the time. This tiny group set out to standardize high school programs on a national scale. They proclaimed exactly what subjects students should be taught, in what order, and even originated the concept of tracking, including stating that secondary education was only appropriate for a small portion of youth. (You can bet their *own* kids were included in that small portion.)

This "gang of 10," as I like to call them, also set in stone the idea that education is a one-size-fits-all institution. As the *Historical Dictionary of American Education* says, "The Committee asserted that every subject should be taught the same way to all pupils."[5] The directives they laid out became the document that the *Dictionary* explains "substantively affected the secondary curriculum for at least a generation, if not to the present day."[6] This is the archaic piece of paper that most schools still use, without even knowing it, as the basis for their rigid curricula and graduation requirements.

Just think if the NEA had asked John Dewey to determine what education should look like in this country. He would have said simple, sensible things, like, "Let's just make sure we give kids good experiences and that they learn how to read and write and think." If you haven't read Dewey's 1938 book *Experience and Education,*[7] now is a great time. I reread it every year, or at least I reread the stuff I've underlined (a lot of which I've quoted in this book). It's not an easy book to read, but it's worth it, and it's only 90 pages long.

———◆———

Call up in imagination the ordinary school-room, its time-schedules, schemes of classification, of examination and promotion, of rules and order, and . . . if then you contrast this scene with what goes on in the family for example, you will appreciate what is meant by the school being a kind of institution sharply marked off from any other form of social organization.

~ John Dewey

Back in the industrial age, which is when our "modern" model of schooling was set up, the idea was that schools could churn out educated people much like factories churned out clothes and cars. The philosophy was that there was a certain amount of information our youth needed to learn and the teacher's job was to stand up and teach it.

We've since gone from the industrial age to the information age. But even with huge changes like desegregation, New Math, and technology, nearly every classroom you walk into today looks just like the ones we all sat in, no matter our age. The only thing that has really changed is that now we put a computer between the student and the teacher (and we still haven't even done that for too many of our poor students). Today, as yesterday, a traditional school is a building that isolates large groups of young people from adults and the resources and experiences of the real world, then expects them to emerge at age 18 knowing how to be adult, how to work, and how to live in the real world. **Society is asking our graduates for skills and fast-paced communication, and schools are still giving them facts and one-way lectures.** Something is wrong here.

Think about what is expected of kids in today's schools. They're expected to sit still for long periods of time, to learn primarily by listening to someone else talk, and, of course, to never talk to anyone around them. Their main job is to be totally focused on getting out of school, not so they can live in the world or be someone, but to get into *another* school. They're taking classes to get ready to take more classes. Their parents hardly ever talk to the teachers or the principal about their learning, and (unless their kid's in trouble) maybe come into the school once a year on Open House night. The most important day for students not to be absent is the day when they're told what they *really* have to know to pass the test. Their biggest projects are memorizing the periodic table of elements or taking information from the pages of their textbooks and putting it on posters. They've got to figure out how to please eight different teachers with eight different sets of expectations and eight different images of who they are—perceptions based on the 45 minutes each teacher spends with them in a room of 20 to 30 other kids. Only if they're really having trouble do they get put in a smaller class, or get an individualized education plan (IEP), or get any feedback on their learning beyond a single letter on their report card. Finally, their education system assumes they are exactly like every other kid in the class and every other kid who was in that class 50 years ago; it emphasizes the exact same "set of knowledge" for everyone and expects them all to demonstrate the exact same skills. **The world is changing—schools are not.**

———◆———

A few years ago, I was looking at an article in *Redbook* called "America's Best Schools," and it was ridiculous to me how the article's researchers chose the schools they did. They said they had chosen the schools with the best overall performance and the best teachers, teaching methods, test scores, graduation rates, and so on. But when I looked at how the article described those "best" schools, the things they listed were statistics like "2,010 students" and "50 after-school clubs" and "78 percent of the faculty hold advanced degrees." The article even praised some schools for having mandatory study halls or great guest speakers. Is this really how we're measuring the quality of learning? I mean, schools might have great honors courses, but that doesn't tell us anything about how well they serve the over 75 percent of kids who don't take honors courses.

In California, state law requires that high school kids be *in school* (no matter what they're doing or if they're even learning) for 64,800 minutes per year. Minutes! And California is not an exception in measuring education this way. **When education is defined by the number of minutes a kid sits at a desk, it is way too far away from what is really important.**

In 1993, Ernest L. Boyer, then-president of the Carnegie Foundation for the Advancement of Teaching, made this incredible proclamation:

> I'm convinced, the time has come to bury the old Carnegie unit, [which has based] education in this country . . . on seat time, not on learning. And, since the Foundation I now head created this unit of academic measure nearly a century ago, I feel authorized this morning officially to declare it obsolete. I also am convinced that the proposed National Assessment program should not be implemented until we are very clear about what schools should be teaching as we enter the next century. Let's not get the cart before the horse.[8]

As of this writing, I don't see any evidence that anyone heard him. The national educational fervor continues to focus on the cart.

Many times I have sat in meetings with teachers, principals, and superintendents who are all good people with great ideas, **but whose standards for themselves and their schools are way too low.** They talk about what they'd love to be able to do and then do the same old things. They just accept as fact that they can't really change anything. The teachers feel powerless and so do the principals. Someone told me about a recent talk show where the audience cheered when a 3rd grade teacher was able to name all of the kids in her class. I was at a meeting once where everyone ooh'd and aah'd over a teacher who said she knew the names of all the other teachers in her school. What kind of schools are we running when these are considered accomplishments worthy of praise?

People seldom improve when they have no other model but themselves to copy after.

~ Oliver Goldsmith[9]

Speaking of standards, what is all the hoopla about standardized tests? As a nation, we are pretty hypocritical about our thoughts and actions. We don't test what we believe is important. **We measure what we *can* measure—not what we *should* or even *want to* measure.** We say we want graduates who are good citizens, who are responsible and can fulfill their dreams and make a good life for themselves. Then we test them on how well they memorize and can answer multiple-choice questions on topics they will never think about again.

Plus, having one standard to hold everyone up against is not what our country is about anymore. There are too many kinds of people and too many kinds of intelligence and ways of showing that intelligence to limit assessment to a single paper-and-pencil test. What's more, especially in today's world, **there is no "one set of knowledge."** Former U.S. Secretary of Labor Robert B. Reich titled a 2000 article he wrote for *The New York Times* "One Education Does Not Fit All." In it, he railed against the use of standardized tests and courses as inconsistent with the new economy. I literally jumped out of my seat with joy when I read this part:

> Yes, people need to be able to read, write, and speak clearly. And they have to know how to add, subtract, multiply, and divide. But given the widening array of possibilities, there's no reason that every child must master the sciences, algebra, geometry, biology, or any of the rest of the standard high school curriculum that has barely changed in half a century.[10]

There is no reason to put education in standardized packages when our kids don't come in these packages. Who wants a standardized kid, anyway? As a society, we embrace individualism, and yet we seem to be OK with our schools becoming more and more standardized. People think setting standards means having *higher* standards, but all it really means is having the *same* standards. Something is really wrong when the standards we set underestimate and undermine our students. **We have to have *higher* standards, and they've got to be *different* standards.** Then, the real key is to get the students to internalize them so they become their *own* standards.

There has been movement in the right direction when it comes to measuring the quality of students' learning. Some examples are *exhibitions,* where kids demonstrate publicly what they've learned; *portfolios,* where kids keep examples of their work and document their learning progress over time; and *narratives,* where teachers write detailed reports on each student's progress and gaps. Yet, as of this writing, only a very small percentage of schools are using these tools. And then there is the problem of college admissions officers not having the time or the inclination to plod through the documentation of these more detailed measures looking for acceptance criteria. If more of us were using these tools, we could spend less time and money developing and preparing students to take the easy-to-compare but essentially meaningless SATs. Then we could focus our energies and resources on figuring out ways to help colleges use the real, meaningful information about a student they can get from portfolios, exhibitions, and narratives in a way that makes sense for the admissions decisions they have to make.

Almost 20 years ago, I collaborated with my friend Robby Fried, now an education professor at Northeastern University and author of *The Passionate Teacher*[11] and *The Passionate Learner,*[12] to write an article called "The Challenge to Make Good Schools Great."[13] Sadly, it is just as relevant today. In it, we presented our "dirty dozen" list of the bad guys in traditional education—the "enemies of change." You may recognize some of these characters.

1. *The Champions of Inertia*—Those who sanctify the traditional school structure by saying, "It MUST be right because it's ALWAYS been that way."

2. *The Sanctimonious State Mandates*—The "if what we've got ain't working, let's demand more of it" syndrome of state legislative requirements.

3. *The Prophets of Self-Protection*—Those so concerned with maintaining their positions that they subvert all opportunities for change.

4. *The Glad-handing Administrators*—Those who pretend to support school reform while working behind the scenes to undermine it.

5. *The Teachers' Room Tyrants*—The naysayers and cynics who hold forth daily amid coffee cups and ashtrays, and who provide administrative cynics with all the proof they need that teachers can't be trusted to work together to improve schools.

6. *The Miserly School Boards*—Those who blame teachers for poor student performance and then cut budgets for professional development. Take a million-dollar enterprise and spend a mere one percent of its budget on research for product improvement—that's "staff development" in most schools.

7. *The People Who Resent Teenagers*—We are a nation that worships "youth" but is afraid of young people: their energy, their self-centeredness, their sexuality, their potential.

8. *The Technical Prima Donnas*—The central office specialists who feel it's their business to impose materials and procedures upon teachers and who oppose school-based initiatives for school improvement.

9. *The Panacea Peddlers*—The purveyors of "teacher-proof" textbooks, sellers of slick and simplistic "plug-in models" for controlling students or "packaging" curriculum.

10. *The Test-Score Junkies*—Those who advocate "teaching for the test" and devalue learning that can't be measured on standardized tests.

11. *The Programmatic Power-Mongers*—The department heads or program chiefs who exclude all but themselves from decision-making responsibility.

12. *The Managerial Myopics*—Those who refuse to hire administrators or teachers with other than traditional educational backgrounds and thus deprive schools of new talent and new perspectives.

And people wonder why it's so hard to change schools! These assailants, after all, don't need to DO anything to triumph. **If nothing happens, they've won!** If you are reading this book, you are obviously not one of them. So, what is *your* vision of the perfect school? Of an effective teacher? An educated person? A lifelong learner? Who around you shares this vision? What would it take to get you involved in making your vision a reality?

The Bigger Picture

I once wrote a letter to Steven Spielberg asking him to make a movie based on the kind of scary statistics you find in the report "A Nation at Risk"[14] showing how these stats would play out in the lives of one group of kids attending one school. A movie that makes it crystal clear how even the most traditional school rituals disrespect, neglect, and even abuse our kids. A movie that shows the immediate and long-term effects of the ways schools can destroy kids' love of learning, and that shows how so many adulthood failures and untimely deaths can be traced back, in part, to something happening (or not happening) during kids' years in school. (Spielberg hasn't written back yet, but maybe someone will show him this book and he'll be inspired.)

Yes, we have had "Education Presidents," and we've had New Math, and now we're saying loud and clear that in U.S. schools, there will be "No

Child Left Behind." But are we being loud and clear enough? I don't think so. If we were, we wouldn't be teaching kids en masse, we wouldn't be teaching them in buildings that are crumbling beneath their feet, and we wouldn't be tolerating the fact that huge numbers of them are not making it. We would see the statistics playing out like a movie in our heads every night and do something about them.

There is a reason why current popular "reforms" aren't working. Nationwide standards are not going to close the gap between the rich and the poor or between people of color and whites because these standards are targeting the wrong issue. **Yes, all schools must help kids gain knowledge, but they must also help them believe in themselves, believe in others, and love learning.** If we focus our education reforms on developing these qualities in our students, then the skills we want them to have will come. These are the characteristics of people who are happy and successful, whether they are doctors or welders. People are only good at their jobs—and good at life—if they believe in themselves, in their own competence, and in the value of others. This is what gives them the drive to achieve.

The ability to believe in yourself and others and to love learning is not "soft." I'd argue that it is a lot more difficult and complicated than learning to read or do math. But it is not easy to test with paper and pencil, so it is ignored.

> The most important attitude that can be formed is that of the desire to go on learning.
>
> *~ John Dewey*

I truly believe that many of the horror stories on the nightly news involving young people are stories that might not have been, if only the kids had gone to a smaller school . . . or if what they did every day at school was stuff they were passionate about . . . or if just one adult in their community had taken the time to mentor them . . . or if *someone* had only taken notice of them and tried to understand what was going on in their lives.

When a kid walks out of a school at the end of a day, the end of a year, or forever, nobody asks him if he can do more with what he's learned than just pass another test. No one asks him if he can apply his knowledge to real life. In the end, he might end up being really good at Trivial Pursuit, but what I want to know is, has he learned to **love to learn** and will he **keep on learning,** even without school?

————◄●►————

A Rhode Island Department of Elementary and Secondary Education survey conducted in 2003 found that the percentage of Met kids who said they "most of the time" or "always" felt comfortable talking to their teachers about personal or family problems was almost three times higher than the statewide average.[15] I know that many people will say, "But helping students with personal problems isn't the teacher's job. A school is not a social service agency." And I'd like to agree with them. I'd like to be able to say that our job is just to get the kids to learn new things, think better, and be "smarter." But in the bigger picture, **learning is about what we at The Met call "the three Rs"—relationships, relevance, and rigor.** And you cannot have a relationship with or make things relevant for or expect rigor from a kid you don't know.

The joke of schools is that we assume kids are walking in ready to learn, ready to have content poured into them. I would love it if that were true. But there is way more going on in a kid's mind than just school. You have got to teach the heart as well as the mind, and for that, you have to make sure that the heart and mind are OK before you can even begin. With so much threatening our students' lives out there, we have got to make it safe "in here." It is nearly impossible to teach a kid who isn't ready to learn. It is absolutely impossible to teach a kid who is no longer here at all.

Questions to Further This Conversation . . .

1. How should we be preparing kids for the real world? What *is* the real world, anyway? Can you identify some real-world skills or knowledge that every child should learn or know?

2. If our society committed itself to the idea that we care about kids more than we care about schools, what would need to change?

3. Have you ever thought about the idea that "the world is changing—schools are not"? What are some things we could do right now to bring schools up to pace with the changing world?

4. Do you believe that there is one set of knowledge that every kid should learn? If so, what is this knowledge, and what actions should schools take to make sure that every kid gets this knowledge?

5. If you agree that the ability to believe in yourself and to love learning are important skills schools should teach, how would you go about teaching them?

6. Why do you think kids drop out of school? If you have known a high school dropout, what was his or her experience after leaving school? What do you think needs to change in the way schools and society deal with dropouts?

7. What is your definition or vision of a great school? How would you go about measuring each of the qualities you choose?

"Unless someone like you cares a whole awful lot, nothing is going to get better. It's not."

~ Dr. Seuss

3

Atmosphere and School Culture

Minnesota School Bans Hugging

February 27, 2001 PEQUOT LAKES, Minnesota (AP)

Teachers at Pequot Lakes School are telling students to just say no to hugs.

Hugging has become a standard greeting and way to say goodbye at Pequot Lakes, with some students saying they get 40 to 60 hugs a day from friends. But the school isn't embracing the idea.

Teachers are doling out reprimands to students caught hugging in the hallway. They are punished with detention if caught three times in a day or four times a week.

School officials "think it's sexual and it's not appropriate," said Ashley Bennett, 12, who has been written up for hugging. "But that's how people express their feelings. It makes people feel better."

The school doesn't have an official policy, but administrators believe the hugging is unnecessary.

"We don't have a hugging epidemic because we've clamped down on that," said Chuck Arns, a Pequot Lakes principal. "It has a tendency to change the atmosphere in school."

Between the ages of 16 and 20, I worked at summer camps in Michigan. I always knew there was something special about that environment— apart from all the trees and the games, of course. We hugged at camp. Counselors hugged their campers all the time. Campers hugged each other. It was OK to do that. We had fun. We laughed a lot. We learned. And the kids *knew* the staff cared about them.

I understand that there have been incidents of inappropriate hugging at schools; I get that there are people who will take advantage of any opportunity to degrade or hurt another person. But of all the hugging that goes on in the world, really, how much of it is wrong and should be banned? **You cannot make rules based on the exception.** You cannot punish students for being human and demonstrating care for each other.

Rules against hugging are an obvious example of how we say we want supportive school environments and then come up with these crazy rules and structures that are totally distrustful and unsupportive. The atmosphere of a school has got to be one that supports learning. And the entire culture of a school has got to be built upon a foundation of respect for and trust in the students and the staff.

Creating an Atmosphere That Supports Learning

I once heard a student say, "At school, I need a pass to go to the bathroom, but at 3:00, I'm an assistant manager at McDonald's."

Come on. What are we teaching our kids? How unlike the real world are we trying to make our schools? Passes are disrespectful. Bells are disrespectful. PA systems are disrespectful. Telling kids that their 45 minutes are up and it's time to stop learning is really disrespectful, and it goes against what we're trying to do as educators. I once shadowed a student at a school I was visiting, and I really felt that lack of respect and trust as I sat by him in class and walked with him through the halls. By the end of the day, I was exhausted, confused, and had the worst headache I'd had in years. I couldn't believe how much he was talked *at* and the meaningless stops and starts of it all. Nothing in his day was connected to anything else, and nothing gave him (or me) the sense that our presence was valued or that our voices were really heard.

———◆———

When I started Shoreham-Wading River Middle School in Long Island in 1972, Leonard Krasner, a psychologist and author, interviewed me for his continuing study of school climate. I was very proud when he wrote in his 1980 book, *Environmental Design and Human Behavior,* that Shoreham-Wading River "may well be the most innovative use of designed environments in a school setting since John Dewey's lab school."[1] One of the questions Krasner asked me was how I saw my goals as different from the goals of a principal at a typical middle school. I told him I wanted my school to be **"a little more human than most schools."** Simple as that. The thing is, so many educators don't even know how to begin to step away from the rigidity and coldness that envelops nearly every school. But what I've known since my days at camp, and what I've been saying since that interview with Krasner back in 1972, is that it starts with the *atmosphere*—changing it and making it the most important thing you focus on when you decide what kind of school you're going to have.

In Joan Lipsitz's *Successful Schools for Young Adolescents,* she identifies a focus on atmosphere as one of the common themes among the four "successful" schools she studied. (Although I was no longer the principal at the time, Shoreham-Wading River was one of these schools.) She concluded that "the four schools set out from the beginning . . . to be positive environments for early adolescent personal and social development, not only because such environments contribute to academic achievement, but because they are intrinsically valued, stemming from **a belief in positive school climate as a goal, not a process toward a goal.**"[2]

> Stop choosing between chaos and order and live at the boundary between them where rest and action move together.
>
> *~ Rainer Maria Rilke*

In 1981, when I started as principal at Thayer Junior/Senior High School in New Hampshire, I knew that the atmosphere at the school was all wrong. During my meetings with the parents, the kids, and the teachers over the summer, everyone told me that the atmosphere had to get better before we could move on to other things.

The easiest place to start was just the way the school looked: There were holes in the tables, broken lockers, graffiti, forks stuck in the cafeteria ceiling. If you've read *Doc* or have seen the movie about Thayer (*A Town Torn Apart*), then you know all about the Pegasus. A kid who had previously dropped out painted this incredible mural on the cafeteria wall as part of our project to clean up the school and make it a more vibrant place to spend our days. Nobody believed the Pegasus would stay on the wall—some even placed bets on how long it would take for it to get messed up. Today, people who saw the movie come up to me and ask if the Pegasus is still there. As of this writing, yes, it is!

Another thing we did right away at Thayer was change the way the school day started. At most schools, kids go nearly undetected until their names are called in homeroom (or until they walk through the metal detector). At Thayer, **we greeted the kids** to let them know that we were glad to see them, that we were glad they had come back for another day with us, that their presence mattered. George Wood described it really well in his book, *Schools That Work: America's Most Innovative Public Education Programs*:

> At Thayer every student is greeted by Dennis and a group of teachers the moment he/she walks in the school. Dennis' voice, distinctive in the crowd, rings out above the others: "Hey Timmy, how are you, my man? Heard you did real well on that presentation in Mr. B's class. What are ya' tryin' to do, show up your brother?" "Come here, Shelly, you're movin' too slow; it's a beautiful day, smile for me . . . that's it." "Steve, where did you learn to shoot foul shots? That one was a brick last night. How 'bout a little one-on-one after school?" No one gets past him without an encouraging word, a pat on the back, a smile. It is the same with the other teachers. Only one or two of them are actually on hall duty; the rest are just there to welcome their students to the school.[3]

This is not hard stuff.

Another thing that radically affects the atmosphere of a school (and also says a lot about how disjointed most of the things we do in education actually are) is the crazy reliance on 45-minute classes. **Learning is not something you can split up into 45-minute blocks or confined subjects.** When I'm speaking in front of audiences, I often ask this question: If you were homeschooling your kid, would you put her in the kitchen to learn math for 45 minutes and then ring a bell and have her come to the dining room and learn science for 45 minutes and then ring a bell and . . . ? Come on, no way. You would do stuff together that makes sense done together. And you would never ring a bell.

I did away with the bell systems at both Shoreham-Wading River and Thayer, and The Met has never had bells. In each school, this had many positive effects, like eliminating the chance of a bell rudely interrupting a good classroom discussion at precisely the wrong moment. At Thayer, getting rid of bells also eased the chaos and crunch of students during class changes, because all 300 students didn't flood the hallways at the exact same time. Without bells, teachers are able to dismiss students when they're finished with their business (within a short time period), instead of at a specific second, when they may be in the middle of talking or listening. By not having bells, you are acknowledging that people know how to tell time and don't need constant reminders about what to do and where to go. You are showing people **respect.**

———◆———

Good school atmosphere, of course, has to start with the teachers and the principal. When I look at schools, it's the teachers who are excited about what they're doing that kids flock to, and it's in schools filled with such teachers that kids are successful. The key, for me, is to keep everything as fun and enjoyable as possible. **Fun and happiness** are two of the most important factors in a good school and, in fact, in any organization. If we can't enjoy ourselves while we are working hard, then something is not right. And, to me, even struggling can be fun and can have some greater meaning, so long as we're struggling together.

> To love what you do and feel that it matters—how could anything be more fun?
>
> ~ *Katherine Graham*[4]

The teachers' and the principal's attitudes about their jobs and their school have a huge effect on the students' everyday experiences. **A shared philosophy** is the most important groundwork. Unless every person believes in the philosophy, we end up being inconsistent and working against each other. This doesn't mean that we are all the same—in fact, the more diverse we are, the better we'll be at meeting different kids' needs. But it does mean that we all need to be on the same page about why we are here.

Educators need to view their role not only as developing skills but also as modeling a way of looking at life. If you enjoy what you do, the kids will respond. One of my Shoreham-Wading River teachers once told me, "**I love coming to work.** The atmosphere is exhilarating. You offered me a home . . . and taught me a great deal about keeping house." Through her excitement, she did the same for me, for her fellow teachers, and for her students. As Emerson so eloquently said, "Nothing was ever achieved without enthusiasm."

I've mentioned the importance of emphasizing fun for the staff, but you've got to make sure that **fun** is part of the kids' day-to-day experiences as well. Why does nearly every summer camp in the country have things like "Crazy Hat Day" and "Backwards Day"? Because these things work! Because they're fun and they help involve kids in everything else that's going on. The only reason I can see why schools don't do these fun things more often is because they're afraid of potential discipline problems (like the kids, God forbid, keeping their crazy hats on in class!).

> To be playful and serious at the same time defines the
> ideal mental condition.
>
> *~ John Dewey*

———◄●►———

I hear kids from other schools who say, "School is easy to prepare for: It's the same every day." On one of Ted Sizer's visits to The Met, our kids told him that they could never be absent because they were afraid they might miss something. When a school is **different every day,** it's exciting and kids are excited about learning. Part of this is building **celebrations** into the culture. I believe you have to make things special for people; you have to overdo everything in a positive way. Most schools just celebrate the basics: holidays, graduations, proms. There's got to be more.

Celebrations, ceremonies, and rituals strengthen a school's culture because they stand for and show what the school thinks is important. The fact that, at The Met, we sing "Happy Birthday" to each kid and often give him or her a card says something about how we respect and honor each individual. Kids don't forget that stuff. When people are singing "Happy Birthday" to them, they can say to themselves, "Hey, this school acknowledges me." At The Met, we also celebrate individual accomplishments. We celebrate every college acceptance. Because we see students' transition from 10th grade to 11th grade as a big growth point, we celebrate it with a "Gateway Ceremony." And seniors at The Met participate in two graduations: one for their families (which most underclassmen don't go to) and another where the whole school gets together to celebrate their accomplishments. It's also a way for the younger kids to say goodbye to the seniors and take in what graduation really means.

What else makes for a better school atmosphere? What about democracy? I can understand why kids moan about not having any sense of control over their own lives. Most of them have zero say in their school: no voice in how it's run, the rules, the curriculum, the way they're treated, where the money is spent, and how they spend their time or who they spend it with. No wonder our citizenry doesn't feel empowered to bring about change. Most of us spend the 18 years before we cast our first vote with absolutely no say in any decisions that affect the place we spend the majority of our days.

To learn about democracy and about how to participate in and contribute to one, **students must be part of a democratic environment.** Giving students a voice, though, is much more than just electing class officers and forming student councils. A visitor to The Met once remarked that our students really seem to feel that they have a voice in every aspect of the school. I know that they do. It's the result of numerous efforts, but has a lot to do with the amount of time our students spend discussing the events that affect them. When we have to make decisions about certain school-related issues or problems, we hold whole-school Town Meetings. These are just like the real thing. The kids (i.e., the town) run the discussion, and everyone has a say in how "town" issues are handled. There is a real sense at these meetings that the rules and solutions to problems don't just come from the faculty. To watch a Met Town Meeting is to see democracy in action. (Of course, this approach is a lot easier in a small school, where you can actually *hear* every voice.)

And what about just basic **kindness**? There was this girl at Thayer—probably one of my kookooest girls, a real pain—who ended up dropping out of school. A number of years later, I saw her in the grocery store with her two kids, and we had this very amazing conversation—just nice, pleasant. I don't think I ever had a pleasant conversation with this girl when she was my student. At that moment, I realized that all the kindness and respect we showed her might have had a real impact after all. Even though it didn't quite "take" while she was in school, even though she was still a pain and she ended up dropping out, maybe it still got inside her in some way. And I thought to myself, she is probably a better adult and a better mother than she would have been if we hadn't treated her as well as we did.

As an educator, you do the best you can. You can't always overcome all the other circumstances of students' lives. But if you treat your kids with kindness and respect, you have not failed them—not even if they drop out, not even if they wind up in jail. There's a part of what you gave them in their hearts. Maybe they're better prisoners because of it. And maybe, when they get out in 25 years, they're better people.

The schools I love are the ones **where kids feel safe,** and kindness is a big part of that. A Met advisor told me a story about one of his students getting up in front of her peers and telling them she had spina bifida. In her entire 15 years of life, this girl had never felt comfortable enough, or safe enough, to be able to tell anyone about her condition.

That is what schools must be about: building safe, loving environments where kids can learn, grow, and experience life. The first time my parents came to visit me as principal at The Met, they couldn't stop talking about the feeling of friendship in the building. It was sweet how comforted they were to see "their boy" in a safe, fun, close environment. I know that most of our kids' parents feel the same way mine did. In fact, the Rhode Island Department of Education's 2002–03 survey of parents found that 79 percent of Met parents strongly agreed with the statement, "This school is a safe place." Statewide, only 35 percent of high school parents said the same.[5]

———————◄●►———————

The atmosphere of a school is so important, and all of the issues I've discussed here are equally important to the creation and maintenance of a positive atmosphere. When all of these things are present, a school **becomes like a great newspaper office,** bustling with excitement, everyone busy and engaged, working together and working on their own projects with purpose and passion.

The typical school principal pats his or her belly with satisfaction and smiles proudly when he or she walks through silent halls. To me, **a silent school is not a school at all.** Dewey has great stuff to say on this. First: "The nonsocial character of the traditional school is seen in the fact that it erected silence into one of its prime virtues."[6] But even better, he says, "Enforced quiet and acquiescence prevent pupils from disclosing their real natures."[7]

"Enforced quiet" not only keeps kids from being themselves and keeps teachers from finding out who the kids are, it also kills learning. **Communication is the lifeblood of education.** My favorite description of The Met is that it is an "ongoing conversation." Numerous visitors to the school have called it this, but my friend Deborah Meier, the noted principal and educator, really got to the heart of it when she wrote this after a Met visit:

> The young people that I met had no trouble talking to me about all kinds of subjects having to do with themselves as learners—and not to mention the

world around them, but also about themselves and about the school itself. And the conversations were like having a conversation with a colleague. And I saw that going on throughout the school, this kind of informal but respectful conversation. The school was an enormous conversation between people who appeared to be there voluntarily, who seemed to feel that this was a community in which people gathered together every day because the environment was intellectually and emotionally stimulating.[8]

———◆———

I had the opportunity a few years ago to meet with Alan Alda and talk to him about education and The Met. When I described our school to him, he said it reminded him of Second City, the improvisational theater group in Chicago, where he and so many other famous comedians got started. He said that everyone at Second City was already a very good comedian when they joined the troupe. But the environment of Second City was one of growth, and it allowed each of them to become even crazier, wilder, bolder—and better. To me, this is a great analogy to what a great school atmosphere can do for kids and teachers. If you put good people in an environment that allows them to continue learning and that reinforces their risk taking, their passion, and their commitment, then you can make good people great. You can make ordinary people extraordinary just by giving them the right environment in which to do their thing (whether it is comedy or teaching or learning) and letting them grow.

Whether it's the grand opening of a brand new school or just another day opening the doors to the same old school, the atmosphere better be right for learning. We are only at our best in the right environment. The design of the building itself must be as conducive to learning as possible.[9] And everything we do inside must **take advantage of everything**

we know about how people learn best. And this means focusing on the day-to-day atmosphere *and* the overall culture that is built and carried on throughout the life of the school.

Building and Cultivating a Positive School Culture

Relationships are the foundation of a good, personalized school, and you cannot build relationships without first cultivating a culture of **trust and respect.** At The Met, visitors are always amazed by the level of respect students show adults and each other. We know that this is primarily the result of the level of respect that the staff shows them. You can sense it in the atmosphere, but it was built as the foundation of the school culture itself.

When it comes to education in the United States, most people think respect is about kids calling teachers by their last names, saying "yes, sir" and not doing bad things in front of teachers and principals. To me, respect includes everyone—kids, parents, custodians—and everything. We must have and demonstrate respect for others, for ourselves, and for the school building itself. **If kids are going to be respectful, they must feel respected.** And respecting them means allowing them to make decisions about the things that affect them and, most of all, believing in their potential.

When you respect kids, and when you make their time at school worthwhile, it is not hard to see how that translates into being able to trust them to behave without all the constraints traditional schools rely on. The culture at The Met is full of respect and trust and the positive behaviors they inspire. We sometimes take it for granted, but it is amazing when you step back and watch what goes on. One time, I asked a student who had been a real terror in 8th grade why she was doing so well at The Met. It was beautiful to hear her say so clearly, "The first day I walked into the school and I watched the senior girls. I saw how they acted, and then I acted that way." The staff are role models for the students and the students are role models for each other. It doesn't take long for a new kid to learn the cool way to act at school, and it doesn't really take a lot to make respect cool.

Something I talk about all the time, and something it's really important to recognize, is that it is the older kids who help **carry on the culture of a school.** A principal I knew was waiting to move into his new building, and I asked him how he was going to build the new school's culture. And he said, "Don't worry about it. When we move into the new building we're going to have an assembly." He really thought it was as simple as saying "Yay, team, you can do it; let's go, school." It is the same way that some people think pep rallies are the answer to building a common school culture. The thing is—a school's culture is *not* something a principal can announce at a pep rally. The culture of a school is in how the kids act. It is carried on from one student to the next. **The kids hold this power.** A principal can say anything he or she wants, but if the older kids go around kicking lockers and yelling at their teachers, then the younger kids will go around kicking things and yelling, too.

Every year at The Met's opening night barbeque, I watch our incoming freshmen very carefully. There are usually a lot of upperclassmen there helping out, and I see these cool 17-year-olds working together to serve the food, putting their arms around the principal, laughing with their teachers—really demonstrating these strong relationships with each other and the adults. And then I look at these 9th graders who are trying to be tough and I can see them realizing, "Oh my gosh, look: Kids and teachers are talking, they're friends, they're high-fiving, they're being serious." And I know *that* is how we carry on the culture of the school.

Exhibitions at The Met are great times to watch **how the culture of a school gets passed on.** When younger kids are doing their exhibitions, the older kids on their panels ask questions and can be really tough. Like, "Excuse me, I'm looking at your journal and there are only 4 entries but you're supposed to have 20 by now," or "It seems like you really didn't do much work this quarter—why not?" If a teacher was coming down hard like this, the younger kids could write it off as just being the teacher's job. But they know it's not the older kid's job. They get that these are the standards the older kids hold for themselves and that they'd better start living up to the same ones. It happens all the time at exhibitions, and it just brings a huge smile to my face. **All the things we adults *want* to say are so much more powerful when other kids are saying them.**

Another great time to watch The Met culture being built and carried on is when older kids do their exhibitions with younger kids in the audience. The younger kids hear the older ones talk about how they improved from one year to the next, how they persevered, how they worked harder. The younger kids see that and then, naturally, try to do better themselves. Because now it's cool!

More examples: At The Met, when an older kid stopped a younger kid from writing graffiti on one of the walls, the younger kid really got that "we just don't do that here." When we adults suspected there might be drugs going around, the seniors said, "Let us handle it" and asked the teachers to leave. Then they held this heavy discussion with the whole school, where they said, "Hey, this is our school and drugs just aren't cool here." The message was way more powerful than it would have been coming from an adult. And then there was the time when a Met student's jacket was stolen—a jacket that had sentimental as well as monetary value—and she stood up in front of the school and talked about how important it was to her. Next thing we knew, kids were raising money to help her buy another jacket. Rather than kids laughing and saying, "Oh well, too bad," there was **a caringness and compassion** in the culture that made the solution obvious to them.

But, and this is really important, that culture was in place *before* the incident. It is not something the principal can introduce at an assembly on the first day of school or *after* the jacket gets stolen. It has to be there every day. In a crisis, two people or an entire school of people cannot suddenly develop trust. It needs to be there already.

The amount of respect and trust that exists in a school's culture is directly related to the amount of **responsibility** students are given over their environment, the equipment they use, and their learning. I spoke with a Met parent once who said her son, Alfredo, couldn't believe how respectfully the students were treated at our school. Alfredo had told her about how the principal had let him use *his* computer to do some work, even though it meant that the principal had to put off some important work of his own. Similarly, instead of hiring professional caterers for our annual mentor celebration breakfasts, we often pay students whose passion is cooking to take care of all the food. And they do a fantastic job. One of our kids took on completely new dreams about her future because of the amount of responsibility she had been given during her internship at a local clinic. In a letter to me at the end of her senior year, she wrote, "In a few years, people are going to see me in the hospital, not as a patient, but as the person who is curing the patient." You show kids that you respect and trust them by allowing them to be responsible for themselves and their surroundings. Kids recognize this—and much more often than not, they will rise to the occasion.

> Trust begins with a personal commitment to respect others, to take everyone seriously. Respect demands that we first recognize each other's gifts and strengths and interests. Only then can we reach our common and individual potentials.
>
> *~ Max De Pree*

A school has to decide what it thinks is important and make sure it is doing it formally as a natural part of the school's life, rather than making it seem artificial by separating it out. "Student of the month" assemblies have to be part of a culture where celebrating accomplishments isn't disconnected from the daily life of the school. The farce in most schools is that they have assemblies supporting the student of the month, but then don't celebrate students' accomplishments on any other day (especially those kids who may not stand out as "students of the month," but make their own kind of progress and achieve their own kind of successes). The realness is in the day-to-day, and it is most visible in how students are treated.

As a principal, **I look at every time I deal with a kid as a moment when the culture of my school is being set.** I know that when I am really listening to a kid, I am reinforcing that kid's sense that our school is a place where he can feel, "Hey, I don't have to fight them; they really listen to us." I am also always aware that the same message is getting across to the people who walk by and see us talking and listening to each other.

The Stories

Everything I have learned about education, everything I have ever said about education, and everything I have written about in this book is connected to a story of a kid or a parent or a teacher. I am a storyteller, and when I start a school, I look for the stories that will help build the culture. Like any culture with a strong oral tradition, **a school culture can thrive and grow on its own stories**—stories of what has been and stories of what could be.

At The Met, our stories illustrate our common vision. We use them to build community, to break down barriers and feelings of isolation, and to share knowledge. As practitioners, we use stories to see the life in the theory. As colleagues, we share stories formally and informally as "case studies" to reflect, to learn, and to help each other get unstuck. As Max De Pree says, "In movements people tell stories about giants and about failures. They tell stories about relationships and surprises. They tell stories as a way of teaching. Movements thrive on their stories."[10]

When you have real relationships in a school, that is when you get the best stories. If you are educating one student at a time, then you are going to overflow with stories. Stories that make you laugh or make you cry. It is a beautiful thing. People who visit The Met can't help but come away with stories, because everyone is telling them—the kids, the teachers, the parents. One of the aspiring principals in the principal training program I helped to found spent a day at The Met and told me he'd heard the same story five times from five different people! That story is probably in this book somewhere. And I probably heard it from someone else.

Of course, my favorite stories are the ones I've witnessed personally. Like the ones that show how simple it is to form a relationship with a kid and make school a place where that kid really wants to be. Carmen's story is a good example. Here was a middle-class kid who came to The Met after spending a year as a dropout from his old school. The thing was, Carmen had actually spent every day of his "dropout" year *at* his old school, just sitting on the front steps. In between periods, he would sometimes go get coffee and donuts for the teachers! But nobody ever said a word to him about coming to class.

Here is where the story gets personal for me. When Carmen came to The Met and told me about this, I made him a bet that if he didn't miss a day of school, I would take him and the woman of his choice out to any restaurant he wanted. And at the end of the year, despite sick days when Carmen's dad actually tried to keep him home, I had to lay out 170 bucks on a fancy steak dinner for Carmen and the woman of his choice: his mom.

So this is one of the many, many stories I tell over and over again. I especially tell them to new teachers at The Met who are just beginning to get a sense of what "one kid at a time" really means. When they start to gather their own stories, that is when they are beginning to see the inner workings of each kid and to understand where the kids come from. That is when they are able to make learning happen and when they are helping to carry on the culture of our school.

Finally, another of my favorite stories is about the time a 9th grader attending another public school came to The Met's Open House for prospective students and responded with awe at the stories of our kids and their personalized education programs, asking simply, "Is this heaven?"

The Advisory System

I used to think that creating an advisory system was the core of my vision for changing the way schools are structured. I now see there are *a number* of critical things that must be in place if we're really committed to creating effective learning environments for kids (see this entire book). But I am still committed to the idea that an advisory system is the best structure to improve a school's atmosphere and culture and make an already small school feel even smaller and more personalized.

George Wood talked about advisories in his piece on Thayer in *Schools That Work*. Here's an excerpt I love:

> Don Weisberger, a special education teacher at Thayer, describes the system's effect this way: "Advisory in one word is communication. It makes the school smaller. . . . [Students] know someone's there for them, they are not getting lost among all the other students. . . . In advisory we don't talk at kids, we talk with kids."[11]

There are many variations on the advisory system, from the way we did it at Shoreham-Wading River, where kids met with the same small group of students and adult every morning to "check in," to the way we do it at The Met, where the entire school is divided into advisories of small groups of kids (I like 14) and one adult who stay together much of the day through all four years. I know that the way we do things at The Met is unique and may not be possible in all schools. But I also know that setting up a system where students have **a consistent environment where they are able to truly connect with a small group of kids and one adult** can radically change their entire schooling experience. It was a shy and awkward but very bright kid who told a visitor to The Met, "I have 14 friends here. At my old school I wouldn't have had any." That was his advisory. An incredibly strong community of 15.

The advisory also becomes, as a lot of Met kids have described it, **a second family.** (Or, for some, their first *true* family.) At this critical time, just when most adolescents are pulling away from their own families, the high school advisory and the advisor can take on some of the roles that are necessary, literally, for the kids' survival.

On a practical level, an advisory system provides a way to use a school's resources more efficiently. It increases the range and kinds of communication among students and staff, and by spreading out the counseling function, makes problems more manageable and better solutions easier to come by. But most obviously—and most importantly—an advisory system includes an adult advisor who becomes that one true advocate every student (and every student's family) deserves. As the (at least) one adult in the school who really knows the kid as a person *and* as a learner (as "the whole child"), the advisor can make sure that all the other school structures are meeting that kid's personal and educational needs. With an advisory system, parents know exactly who can tell them how their kid is doing; they don't have to chase down six or eight different teachers, each of whom only knows a small, subject-specific part of the big picture of their child's education. It is no surprise that most parents lose interest in "parent participation" as their children reach middle school and, especially, high school. There are too many people to keep in touch with and none of them knows their child very well. With an advisory system, parents can be certain not only that one specific person at school is looking out for their child, but also that that one person is **putting it all together.** At a family meeting one night at The Met, one of our moms got up to introduce herself and her husband and added, "We're in Sam's advisory." *We,* she said. The whole family was in the advisory, not just the kid. The sense of ownership and belonging she was expressing over the school and her child's education almost made me cry.

When everyone—parents, children, and teachers—knows that the advisory is the number one priority in the school, it reinforces the notion that it's the child that's important, not single subject areas. In my experience, having advisories affects *everything,* from reducing vandalism to increasing parent participation to decreasing dropouts.

The power of the advisory system has always been obvious to me, which is why we developed the entire Met structure around it. I started using advisories when I was at Shoreham-Wading River Middle School in the '70s. Every staff member was responsible for a group of around 13 to 15 kids for a small part of the day and responsible for keeping up with them individually throughout the year. Everyone had an advisory, including the school nurse and the custodian. This system stayed in place for many years after I left Shoreham. When Joan Lipsitz visited there in 1984, she noted, "When teachers are asked what the most important aspect of their school is, they invariably point to the advisory system. As one teacher says: 'If everything else were traditional, we would still have **teachers really knowing students** and being advocates, helping with everything confronting them as they become adolescents.'"[12] What this says to me is that the advisory system in its most basic form really could work anywhere, if people believe in it and value its ability to ensure that every kid is known well by at least one adult in the school.

It was the advisory system that really saved me during my first year as principal at both Shoreham-Wading River and Thayer. There were so many issues to deal with, but every time something happened and I had to figure out what to do, I was able to call on the advisor and learn more about the kid involved and his or her situation. At Shoreham, we had a kid, Jake, who kept misbehaving on the bus. I thought the answer might be to remove Jake from the soccer team to show him that there were consequences to his actions. But talking with his advisor changed my mind. I learned more about this kid, about how important being on the soccer team was to him, and about how much it had helped him improve even to this point. Once I knew this, figuring out how to continue to improve his behavior was much easier.

As principal at Thayer, I had my own advisory. Spending my mornings with those kids just talking about their lives and their learning was the best part of my day. It was the most significant way I was able to use my time to get at the heart of what my role as principal was and how I could best support my staff and students.

I love advisories the same way I love integrated curricula and extended periods. When I got the chance to start a school from scratch (The Met), I still relied on the advisory structure, but I expanded it and my thinking to get at the real core, which is building relationships with kids. It frustrates me how few schools use the advisory system today, in whatever form, despite its documented success and obvious benefits. But then I think about what happened one year at Shoreham-Wading River, when three of our children and three of our teachers were invited to speak in another school district. These other teachers were thinking about adopting an advisory system as a way to reduce discipline problems and decrease vandalism (as Shoreham's advisory system had been proven and reported to do). One of our kids told us later, "Those teachers said there was *no time* for an advisory system." She then asked us, "No time to talk with kids!? Isn't that the main thing about being a teacher?"

Those teachers, like too many, saw the concept of teaching as being strictly about subject matter, not about knowing who kids are, how they learn, what they want to learn, and how they feel. If a school is truly focused on **creating an atmosphere that is best for kids,** then an advisory system might not be necessary. But if a school needs to institute a structure to help put the focus on kids, then advisories are the best option.

As much as I love advisories, though, I have learned that advisories alone aren't enough to change our education system. For example, even if every school in the United States started using advisories, most would still have to deal with a standardized curriculum. Today, teachers who are working hard to cultivate powerful, supportive relationships with their students (with or without advisories) can't fully leverage these relationships to help students become better learners because all the other traditional structures of education, including the size of their schools, get in the way.

Small Schools

I want to go to The Met because I feel I could do better in a smaller school. Without being nervous. When I get nervous I can't think right and stay focused. Sometimes I'm afraid to speak in class because I think people might not understand how I see things in a different way. So it's hard to explain myself in classroom discussions. When things like that occur I don't feel like going to school. I start to lose interest in school. I feel like if I lose interest I fail. But I wanna do good in school. So I think if I go to this school I would do much better 'cause it's a small school.

~ From an 8th grader's Met application essay

The best way to create a positive school culture, with a supportive, nurturing atmosphere, is to start by creating a *small school*. The research has shown over and over again that students in small schools perform better in math and science and have better attitudes towards learning, lower dropout rates, better attendance—the list goes on and on.[13]

Self-concept, sense of belonging, and interpersonal skills are much higher in students who go to small schools than in those who attend larger schools. Small schools also have a much higher rate of parent involvement, which we know contributes to higher academic performance. Finally, the research shows that small schools are safer and easier to secure. Think about this: A large public school system may spend more than 50 million dollars per year on school security![14] Instead of spending all that money to make their huge schools safer, why don't they just use the money to make smaller schools?

> [In small schools,] the learning needs of students, not the organizational needs of the school, drive school operations.
>
> ~ Kathleen Cotton

According to *Education Week,* 60 percent of today's high school students attend schools with at least 1,000 students (and, the article notes, many big schools are much, much bigger than that).[15] Some small-school advocates blame one-time Harvard president James Conant as the instigator of today's giant, impersonal high schools. In his 1959 book, *The American High School Today,*[16] Conant argued that high schools could get academically stronger if they got bigger. He did, in fact, say this. But by "bigger," Conant meant schools of 400 students, not thousands. It is sad that a simple misinterpretation of Conant's words has led us to the warehouses we now call schools.

We need to look at the most current research and update our understanding of what schools should be. Thankfully, more people seem to be doing this, and there is at least lots of talk these days about how to break up big schools and turn them into smaller ones. Bill and Melinda Gates have actually taken on the call for smaller schools as their own personal mission:

> In less than four years of grantmaking, the Gates Foundation has transformed the notion of replacing large, "comprehensive" high schools with smaller, more personal models into a national movement. The world's wealthiest philanthropy has earmarked nearly $700 million to states, school systems, and a range of nonprofit organizations to create 1,400 mostly urban high schools of 400 or fewer students each—some of them in new locations, some of them in large, existing high school buildings that have been subdivided.[17]

But even in light of this, progress is slow and difficult. Debbie Meier told me about a town (one, I'm sure, that is not unique in its thinking) that wanted smaller schools, but was afraid that too much competition would arise in the community if there were more than one school serving the same grade levels. The town "compromised" by decreasing the number of grade levels per building. The thing is, it now has a school with 800 7th and 8th graders, and a K–2 school with nearly 1,000 kids. To avoid competition, the town set up "smaller" schools that are nowhere near small. Of course, inside these schools, teachers are still giving grades and tests and handing out honors that are *mired* in competition. **Rather than**

thinking of small schools as creating unnecessary *competition*, why not think of them as creating very necessary choice for parents and kids about where they go to learn?

When we started Shoreham-Wading River, we had 300 kids, and we added more every year. When enrollment reached 600, I broke the school up into three small "schools": one for 6th grade, one for 7th, and one for 8th. It seemed like a natural division; plus, we had approximately 200 students in each of these grade levels. After a while, though, we realized that separating the grade levels in this way meant that every year, teachers were getting kids they'd never met before. So we changed things up, putting 6th, 7th, and 8th graders together in three small, 200-student "schools," which would allow teachers who worked together to share the same small group of kids over time. That was in 1972. I didn't do it because "schools-within-schools" was a cool idea at the time. I did it because **I wanted my teachers to know their kids as well as possible, and I knew that size mattered.**

From an educator's point of view, nearly everything is easier in a small school. It's easier to lead a small staff, easier to coordinate activities, and, most importantly, easier to know the students personally. The downside, to some people, is that small schools don't always have all the specialists (like art or music teachers) or the powerhouse sports programs. But the upside is you have a community that can include everyone. As Debbie Meier has pointed out so perceptively, kids will find "small schools" within big schools anyway. That's what cliques and teams and gangs and clubs are all about!

In 2001, public school construction was the largest category of public construction spending in the United States, according to the Commerce Department. Great. But the problem is they keep building big schools! In addition, the U.S. Department of Education is still giving out the usual money to build and support big schools. Recently, the Feds have started to give out more money to break down big schools into small schools. But the question is so obvious. **Why don't they just build small schools in the first place?**

Questions to Further This Conversation . . .

1. What would a school that was "a little more human" look like to you?

2. How could a school go about showing its students that they are trusted and valued members of the school community?

3. What rules exist in your everyday life (in your school, in your workplace, in society) that were developed "based on the exception"?

4. Think of a story you know about the various "communities" in your life: your school, your neighborhood, your workplace, or even your family. What does that story reveal about the community's culture and values?

5. Do you and your colleagues share the same philosophy or vision about your school or workplace? Why or why not? How does this influence the way you work together and think about your work?

"I am more interested in school now
because school is more interested in me."

~ A Met student

Chapter 4

One Student
at a Time

In 2002, Eliot Levine wrote a book about The Met called *One Kid at a Time*. That title is the crux of the Met philosophy. It has always been my philosophy. Another way of putting it is **treating everyone alike differently.** From the way we design curricula and standards to the way we design schools, we must think of the individual and what *he or she* needs and wants from education. I cannot state this more strongly: This is the only way schools will really work and the only way every kid will be offered the education he or she deserves. **Our kids are being mistreated and abandoned by their schools, and too many are literally dying as a result. We have to save them, one kid at a time.**

Too many of our kids are falling through the cracks, getting lost without anyone even noticing they're missing. We were 10 weeks into our first semester at The Met when Julio got a letter from one of the other local public schools informing him that he had failed gym and would have to report to the principal's office with his parents. Julio had never even *enrolled* at that school—how in the world did he fail gym? That same year, another of our kids got a letter from another local school warning her that she was in danger of failing a class. Again, she was not even enrolled at that school, and yet somehow, miraculously, she was still *passing* a class there! This just illustrates how too many of our public schools don't know their kids well enough to even know if the kids are registered or not, let alone what their interests are, what skills they need, or how best to help them learn.

> One size never fits all. One size fits one.
>
> ~ *Tom Peters*

What we need is not just smaller schools and realistic education goals, but authentic relationships between educators and kids. What we need are *truly* personalized schools. **A truly personalized school is ultimately flexible**: student groupings, schedules, curriculum, activities, and assessment tools are all created to be appropriate to the students and the situations at hand. In a personalized school, the teachers' primary concern is educating their students, not getting through a certain body of subject matter. And in doing this, their primary concern becomes the individual students themselves.

No matter how hard schools try, **a one-size-fits-all approach to education will always be hit or miss.** Can you imagine walking into a medical office and being shuffled off to a room with 20 or 30 other people who have the same complaint or disease, and then watching as the doctor discusses the treatment that all of you will receive before sending everyone out the door with carbon copy prescriptions? Of course not! Doctors see *one patient at a time.* It's the only way they can really help each person. It's the only way that makes sense.

I want to attend The Met school because the school I am currently attending is not a good learning environment for me. The teachers at my school don't understand me and my ways of learning.

~ From an 8th grader's Met application essay

Schools that are serious about fulfilling every student's promise must develop structures and relationships that nurture the strengths and energies of each student. Truly personalized learning requires reorganizing schools to **start with the student, not the subjects or classes.** A school that tries to take personalized education to its full potential is equally concerned with *what* knowledge students acquire as with *how* the individual students use and apply that knowledge. The priority at such a school is to know students and their families well enough to ensure that every learning experience excites the students to learn more. There are many great small, personalized schools that do all of this. What I'm saying is, they need to take the idea of personalized learning to the next step: to where every student has a completely different curriculum, based on who he or she is right now and who he or she wants to become.

Central to the idea of treating everyone alike differently is understanding that there cannot be a uniform curriculum for every student in the country—or for every student in a single school or classroom, for that matter. Force-feeding kids a rigidly defined body of knowledge is in total opposition to what we know about learning. Everything I know about kids tells me that **there is no content that's right for every kid.** Photosynthesis or iambic pentameter may be very important to you, but they aren't to me, at least not right now.

On the larger scale, by following a philosophy of one student at a time, a school is creating an atmosphere where kids worry more about *failing themselves* than they do about competing with others. It is making a place where everyone can create and get into a lot of different things and where everyone is developing as an individual. The school is acknowledging (as we did at Thayer, when we put it at the front and center of our school's mission) that its goal is for "all our students to choose a place in life, rather than being forced into one."

This kind of school is also able to create an environment where **diversity is truly respected and celebrated.** There's a lot of lip service paid to diversity, but when you approach education one student at a time, you are forced to recognize, and work with, each child's individual background, native language, gender, abilities, family situation, and whatever else plays a role in their life as a learner. I love this quote, which is from Rosamund Stone Zander and Benjamin Zander's *The Art of Possibility:*

> Michelangelo is often quoted as having said that inside every block of stone or marble dwells a beautiful statue; one need only remove the excess material to reveal the work of art within. If we were to apply this visionary concept to education, it would be pointless to compare one child to another. Instead, all the energy would be focused on chipping away at the stone, getting rid of whatever is in the way of each child's developing skills, mastery, and self-expression.[1]

Does running a school one kid at a time mean putting less time into the creation of an interdependent community? Some may wonder about this, and I agree that it's an important philosophical and practical concern. Attention *must* be paid to balancing each student's **sense that he or she is an individual *and* a member of a community.** To this end, the school must work hard at creating an environment that respects the individual but at the same time expects him or her to be a part of the community and respectful of it, too. The United States struggles with this as a nation, and we struggle with it every day at The Met. But even when it's a struggle, I believe we are closer than most schools to realizing this balance because we recognize that it's a much more important goal than practicing for standardized tests or rewriting our discipline code.

And, of course, The Met is closer to achieving this balance because we are a small school. When you only have 110 kids, educating one kid at a time and building a strong sense of community both come easier. Because small schools also mean smaller faculties, it's easier to find that healthy balance between building a community of educators and providing professional development "one staff member at a time." At The Met, we approach professional development the same way we build our kids' learning plans. Everyone has their own plan, and we look for things that the group as a whole needs. It is a much more natural approach than the one most schools are taking. We give our people what they need at the time that they need it and in an ongoing way. Principals watch teachers, talk to them about their strengths and weaknesses, give them ideas, and help brainstorm solutions. When only one teacher is struggling with an issue, the other teachers aren't forced to sit through a three-hour training session on it.

In theory, sending teachers to teaming workshops or bringing in experts to lecture on adolescent development is good. But in practice, it doesn't connect for each teacher. It's just another example of an inadequate, one-size-fits-all approach. **We must begin to think of teachers (and principals) as learners, too, and approach their learning needs one at a time.** School must be a growing place for everyone. If the teachers are learning and growing, then the students will be, too.

Approaching education and the design of a school from a one kid at a time perspective is a big change from the traditional way of doing things, and it means looking at all the major and minor components of schooling through a new lens. It *is* possible to treat everyone alike differently, even when it comes to some of education's most complex tasks: designing curriculum and handling discipline.

Curriculum

> Don't depend on the curriculum: there never was a course in insight.
>
> ~ *John Ciardi*[2]

Obviously, this whole book is about curriculum development in the broadest sense of the word. If your true focus is teaching and learning, then everything you do—from setting up the rules of the school, to training principals, to working with parents—is "developing the curriculum." Here, I just want to highlight three points that best demonstrate how starting with a philosophy of one student at a time changes the lens you use when you approach curriculum development.

First, all students' educational programs should be designed by the people who know them best: their parents, their teachers, and

themselves. Parents have got to be involved from the start—right when we first start talking about designing their kids' curriculum. They have as much expertise about their own kids as we have about educating. In two of my former schools, some of my more radical ideas came under attack from parents and others in the community, so getting parents involved in the intensive way we do at The Met was, in a way, a selfish gesture. Of course, I'm partly joking here, but it's true that they can't yell at me about what they themselves have developed and decided is right for their own kids.

Education people always say parents are their kids' first teachers. So part of our role when thinking about what to teach is to really listen to the parents when they say this is what my kid does at home; this is how my kid responds; this is what gets my kid excited about learning; my kid's only had one good year at school and this is why; and so on. It's about respecting the parent in the same way you have to respect the kid, who, even though he's only 15, really *does* have an idea about who he is and what he needs. (And if he says he doesn't have an idea, we know we just have to look and listen harder.)

Some may see this goal—creating the best curriculum for each individual kid—as making the job of the teacher even more taxing. In fact, having the flexibility to do whatever you can to make school work for each individual kid makes it a much more natural job. Teachers are free to be creative in the way they solve problems and work with each individual student. They are not confined by a rigid, abstract curriculum that doesn't have anything to do with the very real kids in front of them. In this way, being an "advisor" to each individual kid is a much more natural role than being the "teacher" of a classroom of diverse students.

Second, we've got to teach students skills *and* knowledge. Probably the most important skills kids should learn are how to find more knowledge and how to actually get things done. I see so many college students who have no idea how to approach a project because they have never been taught how to actually *do* things, like make a professional phone call, or network or plan a rally. Plus, in this age of computers and technology, the amount of information out there increases every second, and teaching a limited body of knowledge is no longer as practical as it once was. Motivating students to *want* knowledge and teaching the skills they need to *get* knowledge have become so much more important. We've all heard the saying that it's better to teach someone how to fish than to just give him a fish. Why can't we understand that it is better to teach students the skills they will need to find the information themselves than it is to just hand them a list of facts (or presidents or elements) to memorize? Why do we just keep giving them another fish, day after day? What miracle are we hoping will happen when they are 18 or 22 that will give them the real skills they need to be successful in life?

Third, we've got to use and celebrate the real world around us. Here's another quote I love, from the poet and philosopher Rabindranath Tagore: "We rob the child of his earth to teach him geography, of language to teach him grammar."

When we first started The Met, there was criticism that our curriculum was "too random." To me, this is ridiculous. *Textbooks* are random. A history textbook will leap from one war to the next to the next in a matter of pages. A biology book will spend three paragraphs on the digestive system and then switch completely over to the nervous system. And textbook publishers say kids have to finish the biology book before they can read the chemistry book because that is the "right order" to learn things. Who gave them so much authority? By the way, did you know that in the United States only four publishers (Harcourt, Houghton Mifflin, McGraw-Hill, and Pearson) control 70 percent of the textbook market?[3] If that's not heading toward a "national curriculum"—the exact opposite of teaching one kid at a time—then I don't know what is.

One thing I want to point out here is that even if the textbooks teachers rely on are put together in an order that makes chronological or even developmental sense, that order is still an external one. **The order we should be paying attention to is the one inside the kid.** So if Marcus is into poetry right now, he shouldn't have to read Hemingway because that's what the 10th grade curriculum requires. He should be reading and writing poetry now because that's the right order for *him!* Traditional curriculum development looks at all the information we have and determines what needs to go inside each kid. Instead, we need to look at what's already inside the kid and use it to figure out how to help him learn more.

One of my staff once told me how she wasn't allowed to follow her interests and write a paper on the Vietnam War in high school because they were still on the Revolutionary War in their textbook. I, in turn, told her one of my favorite Met kid stories. Daniel knew I had been to Southeast Asia and would always ask me questions about Vietnam. One day, I asked him why he was so interested, and he told me that since he was 10 years old, he had been trying to get his dad to talk about the war. Daniel's father was a veteran who was so affected by his experience in Vietnam that he would not speak to his family about it at all. Then Daniel started doing research and writing about his father's war. His dad finally opened his drawer and showed his son his medals.

There's more: As part of his "curriculum" at The Met, Daniel took a college training course for teachers on how to teach the Vietnam War. He got an internship helping another local Vietnam veteran build a memorial. By the time Daniel's senior project came around, he had opened up the conversation with his father so much that the two of them worked together to raise enough money for them both to fly to Vietnam. Daniel was 18 then, the same age his father was when *he* had flown there the first time. Together, they toured the country and learned about the war and its effects on the land and the people. They both kept journals. When they returned, father and son went around and gave speeches about their experience. Daniel even developed a Web site to help other kids talk to their parents about the war. As of this writing, Daniel is a senior in college, preparing to graduate with a degree in history and return to The Met as an advisor.

We "allowed" Daniel to study the Vietnam War at that moment, in that way, because that was the "prescribed" curriculum he needed at that time. Again, **there is no one body of content that is right for every kid.**

This story also speaks to another piece of learning that formal curriculum development rarely addresses: the importance of getting outside your own environment to make learning real. The curriculum has got to include experiences that lift kids' heads way up and take them out of their textbooks, their classrooms, their towns, even their countries, if possible. In 1996, one of our Met students—a quiet, inner-city kid from a poor family—went on an Outdoor Leadership trip to New Hampshire, and it changed his life. When he came home, he sat on his bed with his mom and talked to her about the experience for two hours, the longest he had ever spoken to her about school. She said it was the best thing that ever happened to her. Another kid on that trip had a similar experience and described it this way: "I was like a clam, all closed up, and then the clam just opens and out I come, like a flower blooming." And then there was Sonya, a really tough kid who had never seen school as all that important, but had expressed some interest in the history of African Americans. The Met was able to send her on a "Freedom Ride" with a civil rights activist from a local college. Sonya was the youngest person to join this professor and his students on a trip through the South to visit the most important sites of the civil rights era, including the Baptist church in Birmingham, Alabama, where four girls were killed by a bomb; the Birmingham park where demonstrators were assaulted by police using fire hoses and dogs; and the Montgomery bus stop where Rosa Parks was arrested. When Sonya came back, it blew me away to hear one of the most significant things she took away from this experience. She said, "I used to come in late to school, didn't really care about it. But when I learned that people died for my right to go to school, I look at it so differently now."

At The Met, we seek out whatever resources we can—and there are tons out there—to help students bring their personalized curricula to life. We consider day outings, overnight trips, and (especially) full-immersion travel experiences, like Sonya's and Daniel's, to be essential to this kind of learning. Through parents' support, students' own fund raising, scholarships, or by bringing them along with us on our own trips to conferences, other Big Picture Schools, and so on, we try to ensure that each of our students has at least one real travel experience while they are at The Met. The next few pages show excerpts from Met students' journals and reports describing their unique adventures. They are fantastic. They describe curricula that could never come from a textbook. They show what learning should be like for *every* kid.

... I was able to do some serious studying and reflect a lot about how I live back at home. This is where I figured out ... the so-called "revelation." I was walking down a dust road in Potrero ... when I noticed how quickly I was walking. "Why am I rushing?" I asked myself. "Where is it that I have to be?"

It was like a ton of bricks for me to think about this: Where did I ever have to be that was so damn important? At that moment, (sorry if this is getting too "spiritual"), I was walking right past this really cool-colored lizard, and I stopped to examine it. What a cool lizard it was, too. It really made me think, "I wonder what kind of cool stuff is back home that I never take the time to appreciate. ..."

I love times like those, because not only do they make you think whatever your revelation was, but also they give your brain a kick-start, a serious kick-start, like jumper cables from a Mack truck.

I've also been given a much better appreciation for the English language, and have realized, ironically enough, that I'd like to get a better grasp on my own language before I learn another. English is a very expressive language ... which is something I'd never really noticed until now.

Jesse Suchmann (traveled to Costa Rica)

... I wore sunglasses because the sun was so bright it reflected on the ice and made everything light up. The sky was nice and blue, and my adrenalin was pumping as I was climbing up the ice. ... I am the only person in my neighborhood that can say I have been to Alaska and climbed a glacier.

Derek Amado (traveled to Alaska)

... A major highlight of my last few months in Japan was when I joined a street performance group. It was called Daidengaku, which means "big street festival." There were different groups with different parts that you could join, but my host mom suggested I do dancing, so I did. ... The instructor pushed us really hard, but I was in shape due to karate so it wasn't so bad.

The day of the event is still vivid in my mind. Dressed in traditional Japanese clothing, walking down a long road, wearing a large hat that covered my face, I thought about what I was doing and realized how amazing it was that I was a part of this.

When I returned home, a lot of people said that I had changed and I seemed so different. In some ways, I don't think I changed much, but I think I've become more the person I want to be.

Christopher Swepson (traveled to Japan)

... In the second and third week of the trip, we learned common and Latin names of all the coral, algae, mangroves, and fish in the area. This was one of the most challenging things for me because it meant I had to really study hard. When we'd learned the names, we went out snorkeling to identify the animals in their natural habitat. I learned the most during these dives because I was learning by doing. I find that for me, hands-on learning is most effective.

This trip has made my love for the ocean even bigger. It has made me want to work harder in school so that I can go back to places like this to study in the future. Most of all, it has taught me that simplicity in life is great. We had a community that didn't have much, but lived every day with a smile on their faces. I will remember South Caicos and [this] experience for the rest of my life.

Jason Watts (traveled to Turks and Caicos)

Discipline

> I . . . began to understand how to use conflict and contra-
> dictions to promote learning.
>
> ~ *Myles Horton*

I'm calling this section "Discipline" because that's the school word, but it's not a word I like. When you look up discipline in *Webster's,* the first word in the definition is "training." What we know as discipline in education today doesn't "train" kids to do anything but feel disciplined. Personally, I don't think we should even use the word in schools, and I would love to turn around the whole way people think about it.

I also don't like the way we use the word "punishment," because that's the wrong word, too. I know that most of us think discipline is doling out punishment and consequences. But I believe it's got to be about doing what's right to help the kid and the community. When a kid gets in the way of others' learning and hurts the community in some way, we have to intervene with the same goal we have in doing anything else in the school. **The goal of an educator is to keep kids learning and growing,** and so you do whatever you can to help the kid, and all the kids, continue to learn and grow. Yes, sometimes this may *look* like punishment or consequences, but punishment is never the point. The point is not even justice, but instead doing whatever is necessary to help the kid grow, protect the community, and preserve the culture so that that kid and all the others will go on growing. I can't say it enough. If you start with these thoughts in mind, and approach problems with *learning* as the goal, not *discipline* and *punishment,* then you are helping to create a personalized school where "one kid at a time" is possible.

When I talked about school atmosphere in Chapter 3, I pushed the idea that **you cannot make rules based on the exception.** Dewey said the same thing back in 1938: "Exceptions rarely prove a rule or give a clew [sic] to what the rule should be."[4] This is the first step to changing the way we look at discipline in school.

One of the first things I did at Thayer was initiate a long process where the kids rewrote all the school's rules. Every kid was involved. It's amazing, but kids always come up with more rules than their teachers would. After you limit them to the stuff that's really important, you see that they pretty much want the same things we adults want: no fighting, no drugs, respect each other, respect the school, and so on. I guarantee that if you let the kids write the rules (and ask them to keep them clear and simple), not only will you get the rules you wanted in the first place, but the kids will be umpteen times more likely to follow them because they are **their rules.** This, of course, also relates to treating kids with respect and dignity. What you dole out is what you get back. It's so important to remember that a school needs rules for the same reason drivers need traffic lights: so everyone can move ahead safely and smoothly without obstacles getting in the way.

Once you've got the rules about which behaviors are desired and which are not allowed, and the rules are consistent and simple, of course you have to follow them. But when a situation warrants a student feeling the consequences of his or her actions, it's critical that you don't automatically jump to the old standards: detention, suspension, or expulsion. **The consequences of a student's actions must make sense**—just as they do in the natural world and (usually) do in the adult world. If you're going to give a kid a three-day suspension for fighting, then it needs to be clear that three days is how long you feel the school and the kid need to recover from the incident. Or if you're going to punish a kid for being disrespectful, then you have got to do it in a respectful way.

Good educators think of how to make the punishment match the problem, or how to make the punishment more productive through things like assigning community service rather than suspension. But I'm saying you have to look even deeper at the problem *and* the solution. The job is to both figure out how to help the kid solve his or her problem *and* how to make sure the kid and the entire school community keep on learning and growing. So if you put a kid out of the room because he's not taking anything seriously, then your motives should be to help that kid grow by teaching him what's serious and what's not, and to help the community get back to work.

A few years ago, one of The Met's advisories spent an hour and a half helping one of their classmates understand why the fight he'd started earlier in the day was putting the whole school in danger. Afterward, that kid wrote me a note saying how worthwhile the discussion had been and how he'd gone to each student who saw the fight, apologized for his behavior, and explained to them that he was really "not like that."

The culture of the school said fighting is not cool, but it also said owning up to your actions and talking it out *is* cool. This kid's punishment not only had meaning, but also enabled him to go even further: to communicating his feelings about the crime *and* the punishment in a positive way. What would he, or I, or the school have gained if I had chosen to suspend him for two weeks instead? Or, as schools with zero-tolerance policies now do, if I had expelled him and denied him any further learning at all? It's not about the punishment a kid gets, but the effect that punishment has and the learning that happens as a result.

Too often, educators use discipline methods to avoid dealing with real problems. Detention as a school policy is an example of an easy solution to a problem—totally disregarding why the problem occurred in the first place. The philosophy of one student at a time forces you to **look at problems in relation to the student,** the current situation, and the family. It is disturbing to me to see the ways administrators mete out punishments without finding out more information. In fact, it is professionally and humanely unsound, and totally disrespectful to the students.

For example, detention policies are notoriously useless. Yet educators keep using them and wondering why the same kids come back to the detention room every week. And when students don't show up to detention, what happens to them? They get suspended. Ridiculous.

In contrast, the philosophy of one kid at a time would suggest that the teacher or principal first ask *why* the kid is late or keeps bothering the other students or whatever the problem is. Then maybe it makes sense to bring the kid's family in to help everyone get a better understanding of the problem. Then the student, family, and teacher could agree on a unique solution that they all think will help solve the problem.

A student's misbehavior has to be viewed not as a behavior that needs to be punished, but rather as **a behavior that needs to be changed.** The idea is to help a student be involved in changing his behavior, not just to punish him or try to change the behavior for him. In most cases, I really don't think you have to "teach kids a lesson." (Just getting caught is really lesson enough.) You just have to think about what's next.

Maybe once every three years, I get freaked out by a really serious offense. In every other case, I know punishment is an option, but it's only one of a dozen, and it's never my first instinct. Usually, I just ask,

"Why'd you do that?" In traditional schools, we tend to look for the neatest, quickest solutions, but changing behavior is a messy business, and we really have to commit to trying to solve each problem in a way that respects the student and his or her family. We have to commit to getting to know each child individually. No personalized school can work without this effort.[5]

At one of my schools, I had a physical education teacher who was making kids stay after school for refusing to change clothes for gym. When I found out, I asked the teacher to talk with each kid and ask *why* he wasn't changing. The answers were enlightening and gave way to very different solutions for each student. One boy admitted he was embarrassed about his skinny legs and couldn't afford sweat pants. The solution? We bought him a pair of $9.95 sweat pants. The boy never missed another gym class. Another boy didn't want to take his clothes off in front of the other kids. The solution? He just wore gym clothes under his jeans when he came to school. He also never missed another class.

Sometimes you need a really creative solution. Steven had dropped out of his previous school and was on his third try at 9th grade. He was getting to school two or three hours late every day. Rather than just give him detention or some other meaningless punishment, we tried to help him change his sleep habits. When that didn't work, we asked more questions and learned that his mother left the house two hours before Steven needed to get up for school. So we tried calling him to wake him up. That didn't work either. Finally, we decided that Steven would get up at the same time his mom did, and she would drop him off at my house on her way to work. I was already up at that time to start my t'ai chi and do my run. Steven and I worked out together every morning after that, and then drove into school together. He was never late again. In fact, he later quit his band because he was frustrated that other members couldn't get to practice on time!

You could consider this an extreme example, but it's not extreme in the sense that it just fit. Steven's mom was a part of the plan, and I was already into that routine. No principal can do something like this for every kid, but he or she can do it in the situations when it works for everyone involved. He or she can be creative and use available resources to help the student. So this example may sound extreme, but it was really just finding a solution that made sense, fit the situation, and changed the behavior rather than punished it.

When it comes to discipline, another thing that has to happen is that the principal and teachers must **look at each behavior problem as not just the student's problem, but also as a problem of the environment.** They have to ask themselves, what is it about the school that is contributing to the student getting into trouble? For example, we all know that in the classes that kids enjoy, there are few or no behavior problems. And we know that kids enjoy a class when they're involved. If they're doing a project on something they're interested in, something that's real-world related and has real-world consequences, then they don't tend to pass notes or ask to go to the bathroom 10 times. You have to look at the environment. If kids are interested in what they're doing, they won't need to come up with distractions or find something they'd rather be doing.

Making the learning interesting is just as basic to working with kids as making the learning—and the discipline—their own. The results of pushing the usual external discipline can be seen in many classrooms: The students are sitting quietly and looking respectful, yet when the teacher turns away, they start making vulgar hand signals or looking at other students' test answers. At The Met, we try to help students develop their *own* discipline. **We believe if the student has self-discipline, then, with effort, he or she can do anything well at any time.**

Once, some students from another school were visiting us at The Met. At the end of the day, we debriefed with them. One girl, who had been sitting with a group of students working on projects, said she kept looking for a secret camera because everyone was working so hard. Someone *must* have been watching, she said. Of course, there was no camera. The work was interesting to the students, so self-discipline came easily.

At The Met, we find out what the student is interested in and then help her set her own goals and standards around learning more about that interest. Our graduates who have gone off to college come back and tell us they are way ahead of other kids because they know how to organize their time and do their work without a lot of direction. That is the result of self-discipline. Our students develop it because, as many say, they *have to*. Personalizing education means not only personalizing the support each student receives, but also greatly increasing the amount of responsibility each student has for his or her own learning.

So now I'm in charge of my own learning, and I love it. Sometimes there are bumps in the road, but I manage to overcome them, whether it's by meeting with my advisor or taking things one at a time. We are allowed to learn at our own paces, and that's what makes the school successful (along with other things). This school is set up in an unusual way, but it is cool.

~ Excerpt from a Met student's essay,
required as part of the Gateway into the 11th grade

Questions to Further This Conversation . . .

1. Are there any situations in life where "one size fits all"?

2. Tell about a time where something you learned motivated you to learn more. What implications does this have for education?

3. Write down what you believe are the most important things every child should learn. Ask your colleagues and friends to do the same. What is different? What is the same? Are our schools ensuring that children are learning these things?

4. How do you get a student to *want* knowledge? Once you get them to want it, what are the best ways to help them get it?

5. Tell about a time when you were in school and your learning matched your interests. How was that experience different from times when your learning didn't match what you were interested in?

6. What do we have to *unlearn* about traditional schooling so that we can educate one student at a time?

7. What changes would have to happen to make a truly personalized school possible? Where would you begin?

"You have to start where people are, because their growth is going to be from there, not from some abstraction or where you are or someone else is."

~ Myles Horton

Chapter 5

Learning Through Interests and Pursuing Passions

When Chea told us she wanted to study death, we weren't sure what to make of it. This was her first year at The Met, her first project. But we had committed to creating a school where kids learned through their interests, so we said, sure, go for it. So Chea started visiting funeral homes and going to cemeteries and talking to people about death. At one of her exhibitions, she held up 23 rewrites of her project paper. This was a kid who had nearly failed 8th grade and came to our school with a history of fighting and other problems. And there she was, showing us her final paper and just beaming with pride.

I remember that someone raised a hand after Chea's presentation and asked her if she was going to continue this study of death. I was sure she would say yes, as I'd never seen a kid so passionate about a topic before. But Chea said no. She stood up before the group of us—her family, teachers, and peers—and explained: "Death has been in my mind 98 percent of the time. I have now cleared it out of my mind. I'm ready to move on." She then told us how her interest in death started with the recent death of a friend and her longtime desire to understand what had happened to her ancestors in Cambodia, who had been killed by the Khmer Rouge.

I learned from Chea that **nothing you hand a kid to learn will be as important as what's already inside them,** and if you let them start from there, they will learn more than you could have ever taught them. After that, Chea studied fashion and computers and went on to college, where she continues to shine.

Obasi wanted to study all the adoption agencies in the state of Rhode Island. He was passionate and dedicated, and he interviewed and visited tons of people involved with adoption. Obasi was from Nigeria and had watched as his mom and dad were killed in front of him. After coming to this country and being in the U.S. foster care system for a while, Obasi was adopted by a white family in the Rhode Island suburbs. It hadn't worked out, and he had gone back into the system. This was his life. *Of course* he was passionate about adoption! No textbook or standardized curriculum could have gotten him that excited about learning or taught him nearly as much.

Danielle came to The Met sure she wanted to be a secretary. When her mother developed carpal tunnel syndrome, Danielle became interested in physical therapy. For the next few years, she did everything to learn more: took college courses in physical therapy, studied biology, and worked as an intern at a physical therapy clinic. I imagine the patients Danielle worked with during her internship benefited even more than she did, because of **her passion about what she was doing.** Danielle went on to study massage therapy in college.

Motivation, Passion, and Cultivating a Love of Learning

One student at a time. Treating everyone alike differently. There is no better way to do this than to allow kids to learn through their own interests and pursue their passions. When you connect kids' learning to what they need emotionally, you are making academics more than "academic." You are taking the privilege and excitement of learning and entrusting the students with this power. You are helping kids learn about their interests and making learning interesting to them. Nothing I have said about running schools with a philosophy of one kid at a time is possible without this effort to **figure out where each kid is at** and develop his or her learning from there.

Nikki's first exhibition her freshman year was on famed and murdered rapper Tupac Shakur. As the principal, I was glad we had a philosophy of letting her follow her interests, but I was also concerned that Nikki's mother wouldn't think much of this as a topic of study for her daughter's first nine weeks in a new school. Well, the discussion Nikki started at her exhibition was probably one of the best I have ever heard in a school building. Every kid who came to her exhibition knew Tupac's words and had something to say about them. This was not just kids watching another kid present because they were told to; they were having the kind of conversation they would've had at home, on their own. It was wild, but I was still a little embarrassed that Nikki had been studying this for nine weeks.

A year and a half later, I ran into Nikki at school and learned that she was working on a report about Nelson Mandela. I also learned that she had just returned from a peace journey through South Africa, where she had been the only student participant. Nikki could not have handled Nelson Mandela as a 9th grader, just a year and a half earlier. She wasn't interested in him then, and she had no reason to become interested in him. She could only study Tupac, because that's where she was at. She was an angry young girl who was drawn to what Tupac had said in his songs. But when she was ready, Nikki's advisor pushed her beyond that.

By the time Nikki was in her senior year, she had become a leader in the state by helping to put on peace conferences and was working to raise money to return to South Africa to learn more. Her advisor started from where she was at and brought her to a much deeper place.

———◆———

When we are interested in what we are learning, no one has to force us to keep learning; we just do. When a kid has her own learning goals in mind, nothing can really stop her from pursuing them, not even peer pressure. I remember coming to school one day and finding out it was "National Bunk Day." One of our students told me some friends of hers from another school tried to get her to "bunk" (skip school) with them. I asked her why she hadn't. She replied, "Why would I bunk? I have work to do." It was *her* work, and she wasn't going to miss a minute of it. This is a common attitude. And it's one of the main reasons why, in 2003, The Met had a daily attendance rate of 95.4 percent—the highest of all public high schools in the state of Rhode Island.[1]

Parents are always surprised to see how motivated their kids get about the work they do at The Met. Sometimes they're not ready for this change in their child, and funny things happen. For example, Josh's mother came to school one day to complain to his advisor that Josh had too much homework and was staying up until 2:00 a.m. every night to do it. Josh's advisor had to smile as she explained that she didn't *give* Josh any homework. He was studying because he *wanted* to. He had a project to finish—a project that he *wanted* to finish, that he had *assigned himself*—so he worked on it every chance he could. His mom was thrilled.

In her graduation speech, Mara explained why she had decided to go to college to become a social worker. She said, "I went from hair care to human repair." Mara came to The Met interested in cosmetology. While working as an intern in a salon, she learned how much she liked the social aspects of the work and how much people use their beauty appointments as a kind of therapy. She became committed to the idea of being a social worker—a career she said she would never have thought about if The Met's program hadn't allowed her to follow her interest in cosmetology. Mara's mother was ecstatic that Mara had found her true passion and explained gratefully to Mara's advisor, "Finally, my daughter's head is stuck to the rest of her body."[2]

One last story: A Met senior had an interview at a local vocational college that graduates hundreds of chefs and restaurant workers every year. When the admissions officer asked him why he wanted to go to their school, he said it was because he's passionate about cooking. If you can believe this, the admissions guy told him he had never heard that answer before!

> They are passionate about their learning, because they are learning something that they are passionate about.
>
> ~ A Met advisor

——◆——

A lot of the kids I've talked about here are the ones that other schools give up on, the ones that people feel really aren't going to go anywhere. We get all kinds of kids enrolling at The Met, but I know many of them wouldn't survive in a traditional school. A lot of them come to us barely wanting to stay in school at all. One failure after another has made them think they have no potential or that school really has nothing to offer them. But when you can get a kid whose only interest is boxing to pick up a book about Muhammad Ali and intern as a boxing coach for younger kids, then you hook him. You've got him. He's in, and he'll stay in—because he wants to find out what happens to *him,* not to some character in a novel. He is in it so that he can see how *he* turns out—not how the War of 1812 turned out. The right kind of school can give students the knowledge they need to function now *and* the skills they need to be successful in the future. The right kind of teacher and the right kind of school can take what kids are interested in right now and ensure not only that the kids will learn it, but also that they will learn to **love to learn.**

> We do things backwards. We think in terms of getting a skill first, and then finding useful and interesting things to do with it. The sensible way, the best way, is to start with something worth doing, and then, moved by a strong desire to do it, get whatever skills are needed.
>
> ~ *John Holt*[3]

Learning through interests and passions is not some crazy thing we're doing at The Met that doesn't work anywhere else. We all know where it works: in the real world! We know that **the people who are best at their jobs are the ones who are passionate about their work.** It's pretty simple, really. As college students and adults, we are all familiar with the idea of career counseling that tells us to look at our likes and dislikes and our strengths and weaknesses to find out "the color of our parachute." What I'm saying is that we should be doing the same thing with kids.

I realize there are always questions about how to get a kid to learn math if her interest is cosmetology, or to learn science if her interest is photography. For an answer, I'm going to go to one of the great influences on American culture, Quincy Jones, and tell you what he said about this back in 1971. I love this story, which comes from the president of the Los Angeles Performing Arts Center:

> Quincy Jones, a friend of mine who's on the Board of Directors of the Performing Arts Center, once said, "Hey, man, you have a problem with high school cats in L.A. who can't read. Why don't you strike 'em at the level of their own interest? For instance, every cat is listening to that rhythm and blues every day, and he knows about the Top 40 and what-not. Pick up those cats where they're at."
>
> I said, "What do you mean?" He says, "Well have you ever tried using the R&B station and *Billboard* magazine as a training aid? Break down the Top 40 in terms of the lyrics, and you can solve a lot of reading and writing problems. Then, to get 'em on a geography level, let 'em draw a map where the groups are appearing. Then, in terms of the ratings, record sales and everything, you've got him on a math level. You've got him on a geography level and you're doing it all from *Billboard*."[4]

Sit down right now and write out a plan for how you would get a 14-year-old baseball fanatic interested in math. Come up with a project for a 16-year-old girl who's crazy about cars, but doesn't have a great grasp of United States geography. Jot down a writing assignment for a kid who hates writing but loves reading wrestling magazines.

When you're thinking this way, you are figuring out a way to motivate students to learn the things that we know are important for their life success, instead of forcing them to learn things because they come next in the textbook, or because some politician decided every kid in the state has to know this particular thing. I have enough faith in the interconnectedness of what we call "subjects" to trust that a student could study only one thing (say, music, if that's what he's passionate about) for all four years of high school and still get enough of the other skills and knowledge he needs to be successful. If you go for **depth over breadth,** you are allowing the learning to really take hold inside that kid. If it's something that's real to students, and if it matters to them, and if we respect their desire and ability to learn it, they will learn it. **And they will keep learning it beyond our influence, because learning will have become a way of life for them.**

The article Yale University professor Robert J. Sternberg wrote for *Education Week* called "What Is 'Successful' Intelligence?" makes me think about what we really want for our Met graduates and how we should treat them and their interests while they are in our school. I think it's what we all want for students everywhere. Sternberg wrote

> The danger is that we overlook many talented people in any field of study because of the way we measure intelligence, and some of the best potential psychologists, biologists, historians, or whatever may get derailed because they are made to think they don't have the talent to pursue their interests. Clearly, we need to teach in a way that recognizes, develops, and rewards the three aspects of successful intelligence that are important to pursuing a career in any field. . . . To be successfully intelligent is to think well in three different ways: analytically, creatively, and practically. Typically, only analytical intelligence is valued on tests and in the classroom. Yet the style of intelligence that schools most readily recognize as smart may well be less useful to many students in their adult lives than creative and practical intelligence.[5]

What if, instead of thinking of school as a place to learn "math," we began to think of it as a place to learn to *think like a mathematician*? Or, instead of setting up lessons to teach "English," we thought more about how to teach kids to communicate their thoughts and ideas better? At The Met, we do this by focusing on five broad learning goals, through which we encourage and measure our students' learning. The goals are interconnected and applicable to virtually any "subject" a student wants to study. We give each goal a name and use framing questions to help students understand what it means to pursue that goal. Here are the five learning goals as we currently define them, each with one framing question as an illustration:

* Empirical Reasoning—*"How do I prove it?"*
* Quantitative Reasoning—*"How do I measure or represent it?"*
* Communication—*"How do I take in and express information?"*
* Social Reasoning—*"What do other people have to say about this?"*
* Personal Qualities—*"What do I bring to this process?"*

Of course, there are many different ways of approaching this idea, and even at The Met, we are always ironing out the rough edges and looking for ways to improve. But this way of organizing curriculum around interests and learning goals rather than the traditional "subjects" gives students a framework that helps them **develop the skills and ways of thinking that will promote success and build their desire to learn more.**

Only passions, great passions, can elevate the soul to great things.

~ Denis Diderot[6]

Individual Interests, Shared Culture

When you let kids follow their own interests, you are not only changing the curriculum, you are changing the entire social dynamic of a school. Matthew once said to me about The Met, "There are no cliques here. If I was at my old school, I would have to choose one particular group of kids to be in. Here, I am just part of the whole group." Kids who are writing papers about their own interests, studying topics they've chosen, and being evaluated on the learning goals they've set for themselves end up having completely different relationships with their peers. There is no need for tracking, no need to separate kids based on their abilities, no atmosphere that perpetuates ideas like, "That hall is for the smart kids, so I must be dumb." In a traditional school, no matter how big the push to "celebrate diversity," we all know that kids tend to stick with the students who are in the same learning disabled class or the same Advanced Placement biology class. And even within those groups, there is still competition.

When each kid is pursuing his or her own individual interests, competition is eliminated. One of my favorite images of The Met is Carl and Franco walking down the hall with their arms around each other. Carl is probably 6' tall and Franco probably not more than 4'11". At the time, Carl had this green, spiked hair and was covered in leather and studs. Franco referred to himself as a "computer geek" and had an internship helping other "geeks" fix computers at the local hospital. Carl was helping book bands for the local arts center. And they were friends. They would walk down the hall like that because they were able to be respectful of each other's differences while working together in their advisory and as part of a small school. When I talk about this image, I am giving you a little taste of how building a curriculum one kid at a time, according to his or her own interests, **allows all students to be individuals *and* parts of the**

whole. It's an approach that enhances all the positive things that come out of creating a respectful school atmosphere and culture.

Teachers also reap the benefits. Most of us grew up believing that our teachers didn't have lives outside of school. We were actually surprised if we saw them in a grocery store or at the mall. To Met kids, Met advisors are real people with real lives. Advisors introduce kids not only to their families and friends, but also to the things that they are interested in and passionate about. Although their main goal is to meet their students' needs and interests, they are also always seeking ways to broaden their students' perspectives.

For example, one of our advisors moved to our school from an island where he used to fish all the time. This guy is still wildly interested in fishing. On one level, it's not his job to help the kids become fishermen, but on another level, a teacher being passionate about something shows kids what it means to have a passion. So one day, he brings in his tackle box; another day, he drives a group of them to participate in a fishing competition. Some of the kids who went with him to the competition had never fished in their lives, but they got turned on to fishing because of this teacher. They saw how much he knows about it, how much he reads about it. They got passionate about it, too, and the other kids, who were not so into fishing, got to see what it looks like when adults, and kids, are passionate about something. These are both excellent learning opportunities.

It's funny. A typical résumé lists the person's interests and hobbies at the very bottom, as an afterthought, and these are the last thing most interviewers look at, if they look at them at all. Personal interests and hobbies are where I *start* looking. Nobody really expects the applicants to incorporate those aspects of who they are into their jobs. Yet lots of us still include personal interests on our résumés, and lots of employers still look for them, because we value interests as evidence of being a multi-dimensional person—the kind of person, in my mind, who makes the best kind of teacher.

———◆———

If you are still thinking that learning through interests is a crazy idea, I should tell you about the Reggio Emilia approach to early education. In the wake of World War II, parents in the Italian city of Reggio Emilia "resolved to create an education system founded on respect for children and the collaborative spirit vital to a democratic society."[7] Ever since this system was first presented to American educators in 1987, thousands of U.S. teachers and researchers have traveled to Italy to study it, and today there are too many Reggio schools in the United States to count.

Reggio preschools and kindergartens do the same thing we do at The Met: respect children's intelligence, interests, and curiosity and allow the curriculum to be "kid-led" or "emergent." Many teachers have found the Reggio approach to be the best way for students to learn, and most importantly, they **trust kids enough to allow them to help direct their own learning.** An article in *Teacher Magazine* explains it like this:

> Reggio's progressive side can be a hard sell in an era of standards and high-stakes tests. Still, [UNH Child Study and Development Center's] Director Beth Hogan has confidence in the Reggio approach. "You have to trust that children are going to take you to a good place if you let them," she insists.[8]

And she's talking about trusting 4- and 5-year-olds! If we can trust them to follow their interests in a way that leads to important learning, how can we not trust 15- and 16-year-olds? A group of Met freshmen once spoke at the New England Coalition of Essential Schools Conference, and I was blown away by the way they talked about their reading. They each said they were reading so much more than they did in middle school, because at The Met, they didn't have to read any particular book chosen for them by someone else. They could choose their own books, based on their own interests. All of them talked about how they finally had the freedom to really read to learn.

———◆———

If you've ever watched kids when they are playing sports, planning a field trip, or discussing their favorite celebrity, you know **how different they are when they care about what they're doing.** Mihaly Csikszentmihalyi has a lot to say about this in a book he wrote with Barbara Schneider called *Becoming Adult*.[9] In a five-year longitudinal study of adolescents, they looked at how teenagers think about their futures and the degree of influence others have over teenagers' plans for the future. Csikszentmihalyi, a former professor at the University of Chicago, has made the study of what makes people truly happy and fulfilled his life's work, so when he pushes for the need to motivate students through their own interests, I feel I am in good company. From his many years of research, he has come to the same conclusions that we did when we started The Met:

> We may not know what jobs will be available to young people 10 years from now; we do not know what knowledge they require to ensure they will have a productive, lifelong career. But to the extent that teenagers have had experiences that demand discipline, require the skillful use of mind and body,

and give them a sense of responsibility and involvement with useful goals, we might expect the youth of today to be ready to face the challenges of tomorrow.[10]

———————◆———————

When Max got to college, he couldn't believe it when the other kids in his classes threw away their papers after the professors returned them. At The Met, Max never threw any of his work out, because it all had meaning to him. The same was now true for him in college. When he told me this, I realized that, when I was in school, I, too, threw all my papers away after I got them back and saw the grade. Now, I think that this is a great test of the quality of our schools and students' learning experiences: **Do they hold on to their work?**

Everything I have used to write this book comes from my life after graduation. Once I got on with my professional life, I started saving scraps of paper and writings and readings because they were important to me and relevant to the work I was doing. As adults, we all have piles of paper like this. We should make sure that the piles of papers our students create over their years at school hold just as much meaning for them as our piles do for us. **If they're learning through their interests, they won't throw *any* of it away.**

Questions to Further This Conversation . . .

1. Imagine you've found out that a kid you know is really interested in astronomy (or cooking, or video games, or fashion, or baseball, or music, or police work, or whatever). How would you help her go into depth in this area? What might she learn by exploring her interest more deeply?

2. Sternberg says that "to be successfully intelligent is to think well in three different ways: analytically, creatively, and practically." What are some methods schools could use to help students become successfully intelligent in each and all of these ways?

3. Csikszentmihalyi talks about the importance of "flow," the state of being totally absorbed in one's work or play. Think about a time that you were completely in the "flow" while learning something new. How would you relate that experience to the typical learning experiences students have in traditional schools?

4. Did you save any of the papers you wrote for school? Why or why not?

5. Is there anything you always cut out, file, jot down into a notebook, or add to the pile on your desk? What is it, and why do you save it?

"There is no such thing as genuine knowledge and fruitful understanding except as the offspring of doing. . . . This is the lesson which all education has to learn."

~ John Dewey

Chapter 6

Real Work in
the Real World

Most schools are dull, dreary, uninspiring places. In an article for *Teacher Magazine,*[1] my friend Ron Wolk talked about a survey that asked kids to pick a word that best described their school experiences. Not surprisingly, "boring" was the number one answer. Another survey he mentioned asked kids what they liked most about school. The most common response? "Nothing." It is so sad to me that at the time when kids have the most energy and excitement, they spend most of their days in a boring, nothing place.

Visiting schools that other people tell me are good is often a confusing experience. The kids look happy, but the work they are doing makes no sense. For example, the hands-on science curriculum I've heard so much about turns out to be the kids conducting an experiment showing that Diet Pepsi floats while regular Pepsi sinks. This is learning? No, but to an educator who thinks innovation means simply getting away from the chalk-and-talk and getting the kids involved, it looks good to see everyone in small groups, writing down what they observe. Still, the task isn't real, and I don't think there are many kids who really care why one soda sinks and the other one doesn't.

Here's a great story about two units done at one of my schools. The first was an election unit, where the kids learned about the current candidates and their stands on things like education and the environment, and then they went into town and actually helped register people to vote. I remember the teacher saying to me, "You know, Dennis, the kids did amazing work, really amazing. They registered about 300 people and really enjoyed themselves. That was a great unit."

Everything changed with this teacher's next unit, which focused on travel. If you had walked into her classroom, you definitely would have agreed that everything *looked* very good. The kids were all working. They'd each called a travel agent and were planning different trips. They were busy, busy, busy. At the end of this unit, though, the teacher came back to me and said, "Every kid got an *A* on the election unit, but for this one, there were a lot of kids who didn't do their homework and just weren't as motivated." What happened? she wanted to know. What was the difference? My answer was very simple: The kids knew they weren't going to go on the trips they planned. **It was a good, well-thought-out lesson. It was very hands-on. But it wasn't real.**

When we were starting The Met, I looked back at what really worked in my other schools and saw that they were things like the election unit. When it's real work, kids do it—no matter what the subject. A lot of the time, though, like with the travel unit, **the work that is done in schools *looks* like real work, but is not real *enough.*** I have always thought it's hysterical that inside the school building we work really hard to make lessons that look and feel real, when all the while, the real world is going on outside—and it's filled with history, social issues, work issues, scientific exploration, math, writing, technology, and everything else. Why don't we just step back outside? **The world is this huge resource, and schools have to start taking advantage of it.**

When I was at Thayer, I had a real estate agent come in and ask the 9th graders to create a brochure for her about the value of living in Winchester. She was trying to push the area at that time and had faith in the recent changes in the school—which was good, because Thayer was the only junior/senior high school in the town, and in the past, its bad reputation had been a barrier to real estate sales. Well, she gave the assignment to them on a Monday and the kids did incredible work for her in just one week. Teams of kids each had different responsibilities—from design and layout, to finding businesses to list, to researching the kinds of social activities available. When the real estate agent returned at noon on Friday, they handed her a 90-page book—a book they knew was actually going to be used and was going to make a difference in their town. They didn't just look up the names of businesses in town because the teacher told them to. They knew the real estate woman was coming back and was depending on them. They were motivated to do good work and were proud of the work they had done. This was real and they knew it.

Also during my Thayer days, another state made a deal with New Hampshire to dump disposable waste in the rural areas of our state. And so, very smartly, state officials came to poor towns like Winchester and said, "We will put our waste here, and we will give you this incredible sum of money," which is a very tempting offer for a poor town. The kids at Thayer found out about it and went on to do all this research into where the dump would be and how it would be over an aquifer and how contaminants would eventually seep into the soil and so on and so on. These kids actually kept that dump out of town, and they won an environmental science award from the Sierra Club for doing it. You can't get that kind of learning or passion from a science textbook or from a neatly packaged lesson on water purity.

More and more, I started noticing how these kinds of real projects got kids engaged and really got them to learn the same stuff we were trying to teach them by locking them up inside a classroom. Have you ever watched kids work on planning and organizing a prom? Oh my gosh. At Thayer, the biggest "problem kids" in the school would work until midnight helping everybody, putting stuff up, and just getting things done. Intellectual kids or not-so-intellectual kids, they were there, and they were working harder than most of us had ever seen them work. It shows you that when something is real and has meaning to people—wow! Think about driver's ed., too. In school after school, I've seen kids who would regularly miss days and days of school somehow manage to make it in on days when there was driver training. The kind of learning going on in driver's ed. or when planning the prom is real, and it has consequences kids can feel.

One more example: When one Met kid's project was to organize a Latino Night for our local Triple-A baseball team, he knew he was taking on real responsibilities with real consequences. There was no way he could put off the work until the last moment, like he might if he were just writing a paper. There was no way he could get by with doing whatever it took (and only whatever it took) to please the teacher. And talk about authentic assessment! Think about the possible measures: Did he get 500 people to show up at the ballpark? Did he figure out a transportation plan? Did he produce a well-written, professional-looking brochure?

You learn from your experience of doing something and from your analysis of that experience.

~ Myles Horton

You can have a school that is "one student at a time" and builds the curriculum around kids' interests, but the work *must* be real. And not what I call "fake real." The best teachers in a traditional school can develop activities that seem real and get the kids excited about them. What I'm saying is, that isn't good enough. In even the best traditional classrooms, there are always those kids who aren't paying attention. They're sitting there because they have to, but they're not involved in what's going on and **they're not learning because nobody's reaching their hearts.** At Thayer, we let the 11th and 12th graders pick their own projects, and I remember this one kid who was working on something about boats. It turned out that his family had a big Navy background and the kid's father and great-grandfather had both served on this particular boat. I remember seeing this kid's passion so clearly: "Look at this, Doc! My great-grandfather was on this boat! I'm going to do a replica of it." His excitement just reinforced it for me: *That* was real learning. And that's how you get kids to do stuff, to stop going through the motions, to stop sitting around and staring into space. You let them **follow their hearts to something that is real and has meaning for them.**

When we want to understand something we cannot just stand outside and observe it. We have to enter deeply into it and be one with it in order to really understand.

~ Thich Nhat Hanh[2]

The Three Rs

No, not reading, 'riting, and 'rithmetic. Yes, they're still very important, but in the 21st century, they are not enough. They are not enough to counter the heavy issues our kids are facing in their lives or to prepare our kids for the incredible demands they'll have to deal with if they're going to survive and succeed in the future. The three Rs I'm talking about are relationships, relevance, and rigor.

You have to start with relationships. You have to start with respect for the student, inclusion of the family, connections to other adults and the community, strong working relationships between teachers, and open communication with the administration. The quality of the relationships in a school has a tremendous effect on the quality of the learning that happens there.

And, as I've been saying, **the learning has to be relevant.** The projects and work kids do at school must be relevant to their lives, their needs, and their passions. They must be interesting and accessible. The learning must hold meaning for the student. And without first establishing strong relationships with our students, we can't know what will be relevant to each kid.

Finally, **the learning must be rigorous.** Most people look for rigor in the course syllabus or in the number of hours students spend studying for a test. Sadly, some see rigor when a large number of students can't meet the standard and don't pass. But the rigor that I am talking about is the same rigor Mihaly Csikszentmihalyi describes when he says we can "do no better than to call for . . . the opportunity for young people to experience intense concentration in any activity that requires skill and discipline, regardless of its content."[3]

At The Met, the activity is defined by the student's interests, and this fact alone leads to a more rigorous learning environment than you will see in most traditional high schools. When a student stays up until 2:00 a.m. reading a book that he chose and writing a paper on it that he assigned himself, *that* is rigor. When a student spends months studying Spanish and raising money to travel to Costa Rica to work alongside an environmental scientist to help save the rain forest, *that* is rigor. When you watch how our students prepare for their exhibitions—rehearsing and organizing their portfolios to present the best evidence of their learning process—you are seeing rigor. Some people mistake not having a standardized curriculum for not having standards. But I believe we set very high standards for our students—and most of them begin early on to set the same standards for themselves.

We have created a culture of high expectations, high-quality work, and rigorous learning. But the three Rs must stay together. We would not have been able to instill the level of rigor or achieve the successes that we have if we hadn't also worked to create a culture of relationships and relevance.

Making Connections

For kids to learn, the work they do not only has to be real, but it has to be connected to something. Psychologist George A. Miller wrote an article more than 40 years ago explaining that humans are only capable of receiving, processing, and remembering seven chunks of information at a time. Now imagine, as he did, that each chunk is connected in a meaningful way to another chunk. These connections transform the seven smaller chunks of information into a single larger one, leaving room for six more.[4] What Miller is saying is that *information that is connected is easier to process and easier to remember.* **It is only when we can connect something new to something we already understand that we actually learn.**

> In my old school I did little pieces of everything, but it didn't really stick to my brain.
>
> ~ *A Met student*

I don't care how interesting you make the Boer War; if it doesn't connect to anything kids already know, they won't really learn it. I'm way more interested in the idea of kids looking at the concept of war by starting with divorce or gangs—wars they understand. By making connections to the real world students are living in now, teachers can help kids understand important things like what causes wars, how to keep peace, and how to apply this knowledge both in their everyday interactions and in their future as adults. If one student has a particular passion for the Boer War, then yes, she should go deeper and examine it in light of what she's learned. But if it isn't of interest to another kid, then it just becomes a bunch of facts, disconnected and meaningless.

Math is a great example of the importance of making connections, especially because it involves skills and a knowledge base that are traditionally taught separately from everything else. We are still struggling with the best ways to integrate math into our program at The Met, but we are committed to helping our students learn math in a way that is relevant to the work they are doing in their areas of interest: **real math that connects to real work.**

One of our Met students turned her frustration with clothing stores into a project that was real and relevant, required her to form relationships, and helped her to see the connection between math and the real world. Cindy wanted to understand why the clothes she liked cost so much, so she conducted interviews with local storeowners. To analyze what she learned from her interviews, Cindy's advisor helped her understand the mathematics behind the stores' pricing procedures. Later, Cindy said this about her project:

> In the traditional schools, you go in, you do a worksheet, you're out. But how do I use the equation I learned and apply it to my real life? I never figured that out. Here at The Met, I'm working on that. It's actually harder to look at math and use it in a real situation than it is to just do a worksheet.[5]

Another way that connections enrich learning is incredibly obvious, yet it rarely happens in the right way. It's when subjects are connected or when different classes work together and integrate different skills and knowledge. There's a lot of talk about integrated curricula, but even some of the best efforts still result in fake projects that are meaningless to the students.

One of my favorite stories is about a class at Thayer whose teacher introduced them to some neglected elderly folks in a nearby nursing home. The kids decided they wanted to start visiting the home on a regular basis and developed an entire curriculum around the elderly and the issues they face. But the kids realized that to visit the home, they either had to wade through a swamp or waste 20 minutes taking an indirect route along the road. One of our science classes agreed to study the swamp to determine how human traffic would affect its ecology. Then a wood shop class got involved and designed and built an environmentally sound bridge and boardwalk. Boom! Connections! Intellectual, ecological, physical, and social connections! Classrooms talking to one another. **Subjects melding in the school, just as they do in the real world**—all of it involving real work.

Learning Through Internships

I recently looked over my notes from when I applied for my first job as a principal. Now, many years and experiences later, my views on the whole real-work thing are pretty similar to what they were then. What's different, obviously, is that I had no stories then. I had no personal examples to back up my views. I knew students needed to be doing real work. I didn't know how, but I knew schools had to be more personalized. I knew learning had to begin with students' interests.

When I started at Thayer 10 years later, I realized it wasn't possible to do any of this within the existing school program. I began to understand that individual student needs and interests couldn't even be met within the existing school *building*. Thayer lacked the staff, the materials, and the money to provide the broad range of courses and experiences our kids needed and wanted. The traditional curriculum just didn't inspire every student to get excited about learning, nor did it meet the expectations of some of the highly motivated or gifted students. So the teachers and I began looking outside the school and into the community for help. That triggered a formal apprenticeship program, which became very successful. It allowed us to begin to meet some of the kids' needs and had the bonus effect of bringing the community in as a partner in the school.

The thing was, my staff and I wanted to integrate the real work—the apprenticeships—back into the classes, but we couldn't. Outside the apprenticeships we had a traditional curriculum, so, for example, it was very hard to integrate a kid's learning at the auto shop with his learning in English class when he was the only one working at the shop. We knew that the apprenticeship program would never really take off until we combined the real work in the real world with the curriculum back at school, like we'd done with the nursing home/bridge project.

By the time I was ready to leave Thayer, it was clear to me that I had taken the school about as far as I could within that particular structure. In other words, I knew that the still-traditional aspects of the school were keeping it from being as strong a learning environment as it could be. For example, I was still working with a math teacher, a science teacher, an English teacher, and a social studies teacher. My math teacher was very good, but I found myself trying to push her to connect the students' learning to other things outside of math while she was resisting and saying, "Remember, you hired me as a math teacher." And that's part of the structure thing. As much as I was giving her complete freedom to do whatever she wanted, she thought of herself as a math teacher and a math teacher only.

When I moved to Rhode Island at age 50, what I'd run up against at Thayer had tremendously influenced who I was and how I thought about education. Within a year and a half of coming to Providence, my friend Elliot Washor and I missed working with kids and teachers and decided to start a school where we could really turn our philosophy into practice. Our intent was to free ourselves of all the traditional structures and completely reinvent what schooling could be.

That sounds pretty radical, I know, but at the time, there was still a part of me that was thinking traditionally. During The Met's early design stages, I was still thinking that although every kid would have an "apprenticeship," he or she would also spend part of the day in traditional, teacher-led "subject" classes. However, when Elliot and I grasped that we were getting the chance to develop a school from scratch, we decided to go all the way. We focused on the idea of a school where you say to each teacher: "Here are some kids. Follow them, get to know them, help them do what they need to do to grow up and become good human beings and lifelong learners."

We began by asking ourselves, **"What's best for kids?"** and built everything around the answers. Everything we do at The Met is about the kids' needs and interests, real work, and family and community engagement—and we do it well. It's fantastic. We have made the community a true partner in the education of our students—and have completely knocked down the walls of our classrooms—to bring the world to our kids and get our kids out into the world.

The following paragraph is from The Met Implementation Plan, which we wrote back in 1995, one year before the school opened. I am proud that we have stuck to these principles through all these years and in the face of a lot of outside pressure to conform to more traditional structures:

> A person's deepest learning usually results from **authentic experiences**—those whose results really matter to an audience beyond the learner and teacher (Dewey). Authentic experiences, such as work with a mentor at a job or a community service project, motivate profound learning for several reasons. First, the work has real consequences. Second, the resources for learning are limitless when students are not confined to one building and a predetermined set of materials. Third, a student develops personal relationships with experts in areas of his passion. Aside from motivational concerns, a growing body of research indicates that for students to apply knowledge in real situations, they need to learn in those situations. Abstract

knowledge gained inside schools is poorly applied or generalized by students in real situations outside of school.[6]

———◆———

We played with language a lot when we designed The Met. For one thing, we decided not to use the word "apprentice" when designing our "Learning Through Internships" (LTI) program because of the way people see that word: They generally think of carpenters and shoemakers and people learning a particular skill. That is not what we are going for. We are preparing our kids to function in the real world, so we put them in the real world. **It is much bigger than an "apprenticeship"**—and it is *not,* make no mistake, a traditional vocational program. Vocational programs, as most people think of them, only prepare kids for one particular job, only teach them one particular skill. They are just as limiting as programs that only prepare kids to take more classes. There should not be this differentiation between vocational and academic, anyway. *Every* child should use his or her *hands and mind* while learning. An educator's goal is to **help kids think,** not to teach them to be an architect or a filmmaker or an auto mechanic. We want them to learn how to identify a problem and how to follow through on a solution. We want them to learn how to be with people, how to get to meetings on time, and so on. These are the things that every student in our world should learn. And teachers cannot and should not bear this responsibility alone. Traditional schools want kids to engage in real work, but they keep the kids and the teacher locked up inside a classroom, away from the people and resources that would make the work real.

In *Deschooling Society*, Ivan Illich wrote this:

> The inverse of [traditional] schooling is possible. We can depend on self-motivated learning instead of employing teachers to bribe or compel the student to find the time and the will to learn . . . . We can provide the learner with new links to the world instead of continuing to funnel all educational programs through the teacher.[7]

What we've learned at The Met is that yes, it is. And yes, we can.

A few years ago, Trish McNeil, then deputy secretary for the U.S. Department of Education, visited The Met as part of her work looking at schools with project-based and apprenticeship learning models. It made me very proud to hear her say afterward, "I have never seen a school where the internships play such an important role in the education of the student as they do here." This is exactly what we were going for when we started The Met: internships as real work integrated into the everyday world of the school, not as an add-on or as fluff. Our philosophy is that internships are the best way to create opportunities for kids to do real work and learn the things that are really important for a successful life. LTIs are not just about good projects, but real projects and real consequences that are connected to the students' interests and hands-on work out in the community, where students can really contribute and see their effect on the world.

I want my daughter to attend The Met school because . . .
I believe that this school can give her what she needs to
survive in the "real world."

~ Excerpt from a Met parent's application essay

Brenda's advisor at The Met had been struggling to get her to work on her writing and her skills in English, her second language. The advisor got Brenda an LTI at a Rhode Island organization called the Children's Crusade, where she was put in charge of writing the organization's newsletter targeted to kids just a year younger than herself. All of a sudden, Brenda would not leave her advisor's side. She wanted her writing edited, she wanted better ideas. This internship changed everything for this kid. Brenda knew this newsletter was going to go out to every 8th grader in the city, and it had to be good. She *needed* her advisor's help to do what she *wanted* to do. She did not have the choice of saying, "I'm not going to work on this project tonight. It sucks. I'll just get a *C−*." She knew someone was waiting for her work. **It was real and it was important.**

> Students concentrate harder and appear to learn more during activities that they find both challenging and important.
>
> ~ *Mihaly Csikszentmihalyi*

Brian hated that his mom smoked, but was never able to convince her to stop. Then he got an internship in the pathology department of a local hospital. After studying all about what smoking does to the body, Brian did his exhibition at the hospital in front of all these doctors and nurses, his mentor, and his mom. He shared everything he had learned and made his case to his mother in the context of a formal academic presentation. She listened, and she actually stopped smoking . . . for a while, at least.

Chris's goal was to be rich, so he interviewed a young banker and spent a year working with him and learning all about his favorite thing—money. Shari was interested in nails and got an internship with the beauty care coordinator at CVS drugstores. She learned to use PowerPoint to train sales staff on product features and to use Excel to help store managers investigate overstock.

When it came time for exhibitions one year, I asked Lauren if she was nervous about her exhibition, which was later in the day. She said to me, "No. What I'm really nervous about is the presentation I have to give tomorrow to 10 scientists on the research I've been doing for my internship project on chimpanzees."

> I never let my schooling interfere with my education.
>
> *~ Mark Twain*

I could tell you a million other stories of the real work kids have done at The Met through their internships. Every day, another story comes out of kids finding a place where they blossom because the work they are doing is real and the learning matters to them. Here is an excerpt from the LTI section of one Met advisor's narrative (our version of a report card) for his student's third quarter of 9th grade:

It has been wonderful to see Nadia finally choose an LTI and stick to it. She never misses a day and has been very diligent about doing her work for Mrs. T's kindergarten class. Through this LTI, Nadia is learning responsibility, leadership, organization, and most importantly, patience and perseverance. I think that this is a great experience for her, and I am looking forward to seeing the results of her project, which involves working with a small group of students on a farm animal project. The kids will do research on the Internet about particular farm animals, and she will have them try to write about what they have found. By helping others do research, it might help Nadia with her own researching skills.

No matter how many successes we have at The Met, there are still a lot of critics who don't see how focusing a student's entire curriculum around internships is the right way to make learning real. The criticism comes from people who are caught up in the word "academic": Internships don't seem as academic. What they mean is, internships don't involve kids sitting quietly in a classroom vigorously staring at approved textbooks, which is some people's definition of the "right" learning environment. Critics, too, focus on the inevitable "downtime" in an internship, forgetting how much downtime kids experience inside schools every day. If a kid is interning at the zoo, yes, she might observe the animals for hours before she starts to record data. It might take a week for a kid to figure out a computer program he needs to start his internship project, and it might take him an hour by bus each day to get to his internship site. Our critics focus on the lack of "seat time" in a class. For some reason, though, they don't seem to factor in the value of the seat time at the internship— at a hospital, at the State House, at a violence prevention program.

The work we do at The Met is definitely more amorphous than what you find in traditional schools, but rather than see it as "truly integrated," some see it as "soft." What's funny to me is that what we do is very similar to how medical schools use internships and residencies to train doctors. I've never heard anyone condemn those programs as being soft.

Of course, another kind of resistance to internships comes from the big schools that can't imagine setting up internships for all 2,000 of their students. Because I don't believe in big schools, I would reply that the first step is to personalize the place and break it down into small schools. Then, I would point out that my hunch is if you've got a school with 2,000 kids, you're probably in an area that has plenty of places where kids can do internships. When we first started The Met, we were told we'd never find 50 internships for our first 50 students. Good thing they weren't betting. By June 2002, 310 students had come through The Met and more than 900 businesses and organizations had served as internship sites. All anyone who is concerned about a lack of internship possibilities needs to do is look at the statistics. According to the 2000 Census and Kids Count, in tiny Rhode Island there were 500,731 adults in the workforce and only 40,651 high school–age students. That works out to 12 potential mentors for each kid!

Mentors

Here is more from the 1995 Met Implementation Plan:

> Determined by the student's passions and educational needs, his personal program is centered around real work—in a business or industry; at a craft, art, or trade; in government or social service; and on community projects. Unlike more traditional apprenticeships, in which an industry may have a well-established structure to impart the specific skills of the trade, Met students learn the high-level skills and habits that are the goals for all graduates. In the process, they do real work with real outcomes and products that matter to more people than just the student. Mentors are critical members of the student's personal educational team; they collaborate closely with teachers to develop on-the-job projects and experiences that allow for the constant practice of these skills. A mentor's role extends beyond teaching about his job; through a genuine relationship with the student, he teaches his work ethic and models what it means to be an adult.[8]

When people ask me how we get people to be mentors, I tell them what they already know: People love to help others; it makes them feel good. And there are lots of people who want to feel good.

> To the world, you may be somebody. But to somebody, you may be the world.
>
> *~ Author unknown*

But most people hardly have any time. To be a Big Brother or Big Sister, you have to give up your Saturdays. To read to kids in a literacy program, you have to get permission from your job to leave during the day for a couple of hours a month. But as an internship mentor, you are being paid to do your regular job *and* helping a kid at the same time. What a dream situation this is: You are getting to help a kid who *loves* what *you* do! You are getting someone who wants to ask you questions about *your work:* "How do you make that?" "How do you do that so well?" You are getting a kid who looks up to you and *wants* to learn from you.

Why *not* take the time to find people in the community who have the same interests as our kids and get the kids working with them? Even more beautiful is when the kids find internship mentors on their own while pursuing some interest during their free time. That happens a lot at The Met. I love it because it shows kids in the clearest way that their "real life" and their "school life" are part of the *same* life.

Every time we get a kid an internship, we are adding a new teacher to our staff. Who can argue with those ratios? And Met advisors are always talking about how much they learn from their students' internships and mentors. By teaching kids through their interests, the advisor is constantly being exposed to new ideas, people, and knowledge. This is what helps keep them alive as human beings and as teachers. It is sad to me that teachers in traditional schools barely interact with each other, let alone with other professionals out there in the real world, the community they're supposed to be preparing their kids to join.

———◆———

When I visit our kids on site at their internships, I am blown away by how committed the mentors and their coworkers are to what we are trying to do. They are so excited to talk to our kids, to pass on their knowledge and enthusiasm. One mentor had her student give a short "exhibition" at the end of every internship day to talk about what she had learned. Another looked at The Met's list of learning goals (empirical reasoning, quantitative reasoning, communication, social reasoning, and personal qualities—see Chapter 5, page 103) and laughed at how easy it was going to be to address most of our goals in just the first few weeks!

> They open the window and let the future in.
>
> *~ Howard A. Adams*[9]

Through internships and mentoring, aren't we really just fulfilling the sadly overused but under-realized African proverb about how "it takes a whole village to raise a child"? It seems so simple and so obvious to me, which is why the tagline of the Big Picture Company—and the subtitle of this book—is "Education Is Everyone's Business." At The Met, we always say, "Our floor plan is the city." Or as Socrates said it a long, long time ago, "Not I, but the city teaches."

I like to imagine a future where there will be bragging rights for saying to your coworkers (or to your fellow legislators, as one Met mentor actually did during a recent speech) that you are a mentor to a local student. I can see people plastering bumper stickers on their cars that say something like, "Follow me, I'm a MENTOR." In fact, one of our students recently designed a bumper sticker just like this because, as he said, "I want more people to want to be mentors."

When the first Met class was ready to graduate, we started a tradition of giving a beautiful African sash and an honorary teaching degree to anyone who has worked as a mentor for four years. If you think about it, if they've worked with one of our kids for just 15 hours a week, by the end of a year they've provided 500 hours of education for that kid—for free! And it is awesome when you hear our mentors talk about the experience and how they can't get over how much it has improved everything from their attitudes about their jobs, to their feelings about teenagers, to their own self-image. At our annual mentor celebration breakfast, one of our mentors gave a speech about the strong relationship he and his intern had developed. He summed it up with this casual understatement: **"There is something to be said about having the responsibility and accountability of showing and teaching someone your life's calling."**

Internships and mentors, just like field trips and guest speakers, make the world The Met's classroom. One of my dreams has always been to have these signs reading "The Met High School" that our kids could carry with them wherever they go. Then, they would hang them up wherever they are—at a conference, a poetry reading, their internship, the city library, a hiking trip to the top of a mountain—anywhere. And that sign would say that, wherever they are, they are learning, and that place is our school.

Anyplace where anyone young can learn something useful from someone with experience is an educational institution.

~ *Al Capp*[10]

Questions to Further This Conversation . . .

1. Why do so many students describe their educational experiences as boring?

2. If you could have an internship in any area, built around any interest, what would it be and who would you want to have as a mentor? Why?

3. Tell about a time when you (as a student or a teacher) were working on or teaching an assignment that you now realize was "fake real."

4. Name five people and five resources in your community that the schools could tap to help make students' learning and work real.

5. What would it take for you to want to be a mentor to a high school student two days a week at your workplace?

"My grandmother wanted me to have an education, so she kept me out of school."

~ Margaret Mead

Chapter 7

Giving Families
Back Their Power

I remember being embarrassed and actually shuddering when I saw my dad at the door to my 8th grade classroom, bringing the lunch bag I had forgotten that morning. At The Met, parents walk down the halls knowing they belong here, getting hugs from their children's friends along the way. And more often than not, it's the students who invite their parents to visit them this way. Some of our kids even ask their parents to be chaperones at school dances!

Most parents who enroll their kids at The Met have no idea how their lives are about to change. It seems like such a simple decision, but it is a powerful statement to decide to send your child to a school where you and your child will finally be in charge of his or her education. When a student applies to The Met, both the student and his or her parent or parents have to write an essay explaining why they want to be here. For most of these parents, it's the first time they have ever been asked to participate in this process in any way other than providing immunization records and the like. Here is what some of our Met parents have told us in their application essays. How anyone could read these and *still* think that parents are not interested in their children's education or what goes on in the schools is beyond me.

. . . I want my son to have a good education and to be someone in the future.

. . . Sarah's childhood is not a happy one, and being the oldest, she missed out completely. Please help her.

. . . Siento como si esto fuera lo mas importante que he hecho para mi hija. (I feel as if this is the most important thing that I have ever done for my daughter.)

. . . My other son already attends here and has learned to love school again.

. . . I have been requesting help for her since 8th grade or longer. They keep telling me "next year." I know that if she continues to fail or have a hard time, she will lose more interest. I do not want this to happen. She has had some tragedy in her life that doesn't help. Most of all, I want her to be where she gets help and understanding.

So many children lose interest in school. I do not want this to happen to Anya.

Yo ha observado a José tolerar la escuela por ocho años. El ha comprado la mentira de que la escuela tiene que ser tolerada para hacer cosas divertidas. Yo quiero que el se divierta en el prendizaje. (I have watched José tolerate school for eight years. He has bought the lie that school is to be tolerated to get to the fun stuff. I want him to experience the fun in learning.)

I'd just like a chance to see him grow and prosper for the community, his race, and his family name. And, most importantly, his self!

Yes, it takes a lot of work to truly engage families in their children's education, but how could anyone ignore these voices of parents who have every right to demand inclusion?

"We Enroll Families"

At The Met, parents are involved from the first step to the last. They write their application essays, and then, when their child actually enrolls, we consider them "enrolled," too. The title of this section is one of our Met mottos. First, parents become members of their child's Learning Plan Team, alongside their child, his or her internship mentor, and his or her advisor. Every quarter, they serve as panel members at their child's exhibition and are asked to give critical feedback on their child's progress. Finally, at the end of the four years, exhausted and elated from their intense participation, the parents get up in front of the school and sign their child's diploma, along with the principal, the board chairman, and the state commissioner of education. Some of these parents never graduated from high school themselves; some have watched family members die on the streets of Providence or in their home countries; many weren't sure if their child would even return to school after being kicked out or dropping out of other districts. And many are about to watch their child become the first member of their family to go to college.

Met staff receive lots of incredible cards and letters from parents. I remember the card one of our guidance counselors received from a parent who had ended up in prison and had just found out she was going to be paroled in a few months. The counselor had stayed in contact with this mother and her children, and the mother had written to thank her. She wrote, "You have taught me I do have someone who really cares. You are a beautiful person and a true friend. When I get out, I'm really looking forward to talking to you and seeing you."

Another parent expressed her gratitude to The Met by writing to our weekly family newsletter:

> I greatly appreciate the staff at The Met's willingness to communicate about difficult issues that impact kids. They are hanging in through some big bumps in the road for us as a family. I feel heard and supported. It is such a huge contrast from other schools my children have attended. Thank you so much!!!

These powerful statements reflect the deep effect that true family engagement can have on parents, staff, students, and the culture of the school. Over and over again, I've seen The Met transform entire families by helping parents take control not only of their child's education, but also of their own lives—some for the first time.

———◆———

I have spent a lot of time listening to parents and asking them what they want for their children. And, of course, I also read everything I can get my hands on about education. I have been profoundly affected by what I've read on family and community involvement in schools. For example, I believe it was Norman Cousins, former editor of the *Saturday Review* (1937–1972), who asked, "Who took the 'public' out of public schools?" Ivan Illich's entire book, *Deschooling Society,* asks, "Who said that professional educators are the only ones who can educate our kids?" Seymour Sarason writes about how **education will not change until we change the power structure.** According to Seymour, as long as the same people are making all the decisions, everything will stay pretty much the same. One of his main arguments has been that we'll only really change our education system when we extend decision making down to the next level, to the community and to the parents.

All of these writers and many, many more have influenced my thinking about who "owns" education, how a school can be truly democratic, what kind of role parents can play, how a school can take the current definition of "parent involvement" to the next level, and so on. When we started The Met, I wanted parents to be involved in the real decisions that affect them and their kids. Every parent has opinions about their child's education, but most don't have an outlet to say or do anything about it. When parents choose The Met for their child, I want them to know that their opinions matter. So over the years, in addition to asking parents to help determine their child's total curriculum, we have asked them to help us make schoolwide decisions ranging from what time school should start in the mornings to whether students should call teachers by their first names (our parents said yes). To me, the commitment is to keep finding ways to **involve parents in the real decisions we make every day** about the school.

———◆———

I don't talk much these days about my first job in 1969 in the Ocean Hill-Brownsville district in Brooklyn, New York. But after watching the full 20 minutes dedicated to that same place and time in the film *Eyes on the Prize,* I gained a new perspective on how my experiences there contributed to what we're doing now at The Met. Back in '69, when I was only 25 years old, I was using education to fight for the civil rights of poor black kids and their parents. Ocean Hill-Brownsville was the first community-controlled district in the country; lots of other cities went on to use it as a model for breaking down their large, bureaucratic districts and returning control of the schools to local people. So really, way back then, I was already thinking about broadening the definition of "parent involvement."

Soon after that experience in Brooklyn, I started Shoreham-Wading River Middle School on Long Island and immediately set up neighborhood groups. Here's an overview of what we did, from Joan Lipsitz's account in her book *Successful Schools for Young Adolescents:*

> In one of his most inspired moves, Littky divided the school district into 16 zones. He established a Parent Liaison Committee with one chairperson for each zone in order that every neighborhood would have a parent representative. This communications network became his mouthpiece and his ears. Meeting one time monthly, the parents were oriented to how and why the school functioned as it did. Each representative spent half a day in school, observing and learning. At meetings, they came with comments and questions from their zones, concerns people would not communicate directly

to the school but were willing to discuss with a neighbor. Representatives called to remind families in their zones about important meetings and budget votes. The chairperson from each zone was given a loose-leaf notebook with curricular goals from every class, a district calendar, a suggested script for his or her first phone calls in the zone, community information for new families, a handbook about school policies, the middle school's philosophy statement, the year's list of advisories, sample schedules, and curricular overviews by teams. The Parent Liaison Committee still functions as a successful communication link that scotches rumors, advocates for the school at board meetings and for parents at school meetings, and advises the administration about issues of current concern in the school. Open houses, parent tours, questionnaires at parent-teacher conferences through which parents could express their feelings about the school, invitations to parents to go on field trips, the parent council—all helped convince the parents that the red-bearded rebel knew what he was doing. Classes for parents about pre- and early adolescent development helped parents understand the school and gave them a forum for sharing what they thought were isolated child-rearing experiences. Parents read Fritz Redl and Charity James on the needs of young adolescents and school philosophy. They read John Dewey to connect philosophy with specific school practices.[1]

In this book, Lipsitz writes that the parents are the "red-bearded rebel's" legacy. I am very proud of that. While my beard is now gray, it is sad to me that I am still so often considered a rebel when it comes to fighting for parents' inclusion in their children's education.

◆

When I left Shoreham and became the principal of Thayer, one of my first big moves was parent outreach. Everyone really knocked the parents at Thayer, saying that they didn't care, they never came in, they didn't do this or that. Winchester was a really poor town, heavy on trailer parks, heavy on single-parent families. It was also a small town like many, meaning that high school athletics were a big deal to almost everybody in the community. Thayer was a strong sports school with a particularly popular and talented basketball team. I saw the challenge as getting everybody in Winchester as interested and involved in other aspects of our school as they were in our sports program. So I began organizing pregame pep rallies and using them to show off the accomplishments our kids were making outside of athletics. Everyone would file in to the gym for the pep rally, and I'd have them sit and listen as kids read poetry, showed their history projects, and presented exhibitions of their work. *Then* I would bring the team out onto the court.

Also at Thayer, with the first report card day approaching, I did this big campaign to get the parents to come in, pick up their kids' report cards in person, and meet their kids' teachers and me. I began by negotiating with the teachers union to take the first "teacher conference" day and turn it into a "parent conference" day. Then, I appealed to the local employers to allow parents time off to attend. During American Education Week (whatever *that* means), I sent out letters to every business from McDonald's to factories saying, "This is American Education Week. Would you please allow your workers who have children at Thayer to come in for one hour and meet with the teachers?" I also made it clear that I would not give out report cards if parents didn't come in.

The big day came, and attendance was incredible: Over 98 percent of parents showed up. That parent conference day marked the first time the **parents were really seen as integral to the educational process,** and it changed everything we did from then on. I was so excited about the turnout that I decided to go further. I got the word out, and we started this great parent group where (like at Shoreham) interested parents and I would get together and read John Dewey, take the standardized tests their kids would be taking, and just generally deconstruct the whole idea of who "owns" a child's education. I looked at my job then, as I do today, as helping to educate parents about education and helping them to become true partners in the process—both in the little picture of their own child and in the big picture of the entire education system. It's about putting the power back into their hands.

———◆———

After I left Thayer, and before I moved to Rhode Island, I traveled for six months. I spent most of that time in third world countries that didn't have schools, and the way that I saw kids being brought up just seemed so much healthier than the way we do it here in the United States. No matter what their age, kids were *with* their parents—at their workplaces or wherever they were—all day long. If the mothers were making something someplace, the kids were by their sides watching and, of course, learning. In those countries, I didn't see that split between kids and adults that we have in this country. The kids and adults did stuff together. These experiences led me to take what I'd been doing with parents to a whole new level when we started The Met. It led me to value the kid-parent relationship even more and to realize how important it is to make this a bigger priority in how we do schools in the States.

For lots of educators, my way is a different way of thinking. Too many capital "E" educators think the less parent involvement, the better. I remember sitting in on a principal's meeting with parents and the principal saying to me afterward, "Pretty good, huh? I used all these big words and I talked for a long time above them, so that nobody would have any questions or understand what I meant." *He actually said this to me*. It was a perfect example of the wrong way of thinking: that parents are the amateurs and school people are the professionals. That school people know what is right for kids, and parents just get in the way. And to that, I respond, **who are we to make decisions for other people's kids?**

The hardest-working teachers with the best of intentions could never fully respond to the individual requests, questions, and demands of the parents of the more than 150 kids they work with every day. The traditional school structure works against parents and teachers collaborating, and even causes antagonism between the two. This in turn disempowers families, which is a particularly significant problem for parents who are already disempowered by virtue of poverty, race, ethnicity, or native language. It's why I push so hard for small schools and the advisory structure.

A large part of our staff training at The Met involves teaching the skills and providing the tools to really engage families in the life of our school, things like how to be good listeners; how to ask probing questions; how to gather information to understand the child, his home, his culture and his community; and how to ask for parents' help and collaboration in providing the best possible education for their children. A kid once said to me, "I don't like it, because I can't trick them [my parents and advisor] or play them off of each other, but I know it's good for me that they are always talking to each other about me and my work." **Engaging families in education engages each student and activates a built-in support system that works to help both students and teachers do a better job.**

Some people think we do all this "family engagement" stuff at The Met because it's "cool." Yes, it *is* cool, but we're doing it because we've learned that it is the best way to do what we do better. We are always quizzing parents to get ideas for what else we can do to help their kids succeed in our school and in life. I've known the kids for six months, or one day, or two years—but their parents have known them all their lives!

Questions Parents Should Ask About Their School

> What the best and wisest parent wants for his own child, that must be what the community wants for all its children.
>
> *~ John Dewey*

In the past 30 years, I have written several articles attempting to show parents how to take control of their children's education, even if the school doesn't directly invite them to do so. In one series of articles, published in New Hampshire's *Keene Sentinel* in 1979, I encouraged parents to spend a few hours or an entire day at their child's school observing and using some guiding questions to help focus their observations. Take a look at these questions and imagine what the answers would be at your school—or your child's school.

First, some questions about, and for, the principal. Parents need to understand that although the teachers are important, the superintendent is important, and the board of education is important, every school takes on the personality, the style, and the standards of its principal. The principal is the head of the household. He or she sets rules, sees that those rules are carried out, and puts money in the budget for programs he or she likes. Most important, the principal sets the tone, the attitude, and the atmosphere of the school, and determines the influence teachers can have. Parents, find out the answers to these questions:

* How often does your child see the principal?
* Where does he or she see the principal? In the halls? In the classroom?
* Does the principal know your child? Your child's friends? Does the principal talk with them? Know their names?
* Does the principal make an appearance at school dances or sports events?
* What does your child think is important to the principal? Clean halls? Good grades? That learning is fun? That students speak out? That students are quiet?
* Do the teachers teach differently when the principal walks into their classroom?
* What does the principal do when he or she walks into a classroom? Sit and watch? Participate?
* What do you think the teachers think of the principal? How can you tell?
* Do *you* respect the principal? Why or why not?

Few parents feel comfortable just going in to talk with their child's principal. Sitting in the principal's office shouldn't be a scary experience, but for a lot of parents, it is. ("Dennis Littky! Report to the principal's office!") To take control of their children's education, though, parents must take control of their relationship with the principal. They should feel free to ask the principal questions like these:

* What are his or her goals for the year? Are these goals general and vague, or clear and specific?
* How does he or she feel about being a principal? About being the principal of this school?
* How is he or she trying to improve the school?

* How does he or she work with staff? Does he or she direct staff to help each other?
* Does he or she ever call in outside resources (like local community agencies) to support the school's activities and the students?
* What steps is he or she taking to help teachers become better at what they do?
* How does he or she view discipline? Whose problem is it?
* What does he or she do during a typical school day? Does it include spending time with students? With teachers? Or is the time spent mostly doing paperwork and only responding when there is a crisis?
* Does he or she want to hear *parents'* ideas about how to improve parent engagement in the school?

Now, here are some general questions parents should consider about the school:

* Does the school put a priority on doing well, or is it "uncool" to get good grades?
* Does the school reward hard work, or does it give students the impression that no one cares either way?
* What clues are the teachers giving about the world of work? About honesty? About responsibility? About caring for other people?
* Does the school allow students to speak out and to learn to stand on their own?
* Does the school offer choices and encourage decision making?

Parents should visit their children's schools, and not just on parents nights or when their kids are in trouble. If you are a parent, when you are at the school, be sure to look at all the students (not just at your own kid, about whom you might not be able to be so objective) and then think about questions like these:

* Do the kids look bored? Scared? Disinterested? Involved? Curious?
* Are *you* bored?
* Are students wandering aimlessly in the halls?
* Do the kids seem to care about each other?
* Who is answering the questions in class? A few students? Many?

* What are the uninvolved or silent students doing when others are participating or answering questions?
* Do the students seem to respect the teachers?
* Do the teachers have to keep telling the students to be quiet or to listen?
* Are the teachers doing all the talking?

At schools with a traditional class/bell structure, the time between classes reveals a lot about the culture of the school:

* Do the students seem to see this time as their five minutes of freedom?
* Where are the teachers during class changes? Do they seem like guards? Are they hiding? Do they seem to be interacting with students? If they are interacting, do they seem to be really listening and paying attention to students, or are they just nodding and moving on?
* Is the principal around? How is he or she interacting with the students? Do students seem to be avoiding the principal?

Open communication between parents and teachers is so important to a good school. Most teachers only set aside significant time for parents whose kids are not doing well. Parents, make it a point to talk to your kids' teachers and ask them

* What is the best thing about the school?
* Is the school supportive of their work?
* What are the problems, and, more importantly, how are the problems solved?
* Do they feel that they're part of the process of problem solving and policymaking, or are these things solely the principal's job?
* Do they and the other teachers care mainly about their own classes? What work do they do that is focused on the whole school?
* Are they proud of their school?

Finding the answers to these questions gives parents a good start at figuring out what needs to change at a school, but no parent can make the changes a school needs without the commitment of the teachers and principals. And parents, teachers, and principals can't work together unless they are really communicating. At The Met, even with all we are doing, we are still just beginning to really learn how to get and keep parents engaged in education. It must be a two-way street. It is hard work on both ends, but what we've seen so far has convinced me that it is so worth it.

———◆———

One of my favorite memories of The Met's first years is of a unique kind of parents night. We had been struggling to improve parents' understanding of how exhibitions worked and to build a culture where the parents were present at every one of their children's exhibitions. So we invited parents to give their own exhibitions! It was so moving, and you could see how proud the moms and dads were of themselves and of the work they had done. I remember Santos's mother struggling through her presentation in English and then giving it again in Spanish. Roberta and Carla's mother taught us about inventory, and Dianna's mother explained how radiation works on cancer patients. Laura's parents bragged about their volunteer ambulance, and Raman's mother smiled proudly as she showed off her architectural drawings.

Every year, we add new structures and traditions that keep our parents engaged in their child's education and the life of the school. For our new families, we started a buddy program that matches them with a "veteran" family who shows them the ropes and helps us to carry on the culture. One of our newest traditions is "Empty Nest" nights, where parents of graduates come together to talk about issues they face now that their kids are in college. From the day they decide to enroll their child in our school, Met families **know that we want and need their input, even beyond graduation.** And, as I've said, many of them get far more from the experience than they'd ever hoped for. As one parent wrote in our weekly newsletter, "Can I just say that The Met has opened me up? I took The Met philosophy of speaking up for what interests me and made it a part of my life."

Questions to Further This Conversation . . .

1. Name three reasons why a parent would be interested in, or even excited about, being involved in their child's education.

2. Now name three ways a school could engage this parent.

3. Why do schools so often seem to resist, or even fear, parent involvement? What can parents do to change this? What can schools do?

4. How are parents traditionally included in determining how schools educate their children? How could we go about changing this to "give parents back their power"?

5. In what ways are teachers the amateurs and parents the experts?

"I'm not a letter in the alphabet. I'm more than that."

~ A Met student

8

Measuring What Matters in a Way That Matters

A student once came to me at the end of the summer with a report from his middle school to prove that he had passed the 8th grade summer school program. What he handed me was unbelievable. On a slip of paper a quarter-inch high and 11-inches wide was his name, the name of the school, whether he took summer school for math or English, and a check in the box marked "Pass."

This is what his school was using to tell me about what kind of kid he was. This is what today's schools consider an acceptable evaluation tool. This, plus millions of slightly larger pieces of paper that use single letter grades to describe weeks and weeks of our children's lives. I find this lazy, disrespectful, and completely unacceptable. As educators, we ask kids to produce pages and pages of words, and then we only take the time to write one letter to help them see how they've progressed and what they need to do to improve. *A. B. C. D. F.* It's pathetic.

Grades vs. Narratives

Schools use grades because it's one of those things somebody once decided on and now everybody just goes along with it. I don't know where it started, but I know where it stops—in the real world. You don't see supervisors telling their employees, "Great job, I'm going to give you an *A*." Or, "You really screwed up here; that's a *C–*." No, in the real world, **adults get real feedback** and indications of where they need improvement. If you were the communications director for a company and you had to present your team's annual report to the board of directors, at the end of the meeting, the board members would not shake your hand and say, "Nice work, Dennis, we're gonna give you a *B+* on that one." They'd talk about what was good and where you were lacking the information they needed. They'd tell you that you didn't develop a plan of action here or show your data there. And when you went ahead and brought them the stuff they'd asked for, they wouldn't say, "Oh, OK, Dennis, big improvement. You now get an *A–*."

In the real world, when we evaluate things, we talk about the specifics of what is right and what is wrong. A baseball coach doesn't say to his player, "You earned a *B* today." He says, "You took your eye off the ball today. You need to concentrate more. You need to change your stance." **The real world is built around giving feedback and showing people what they need to do to improve.** And yet in schools, we hand out single-letter grades and think nothing of it.

The really awful thing is that, in most schools, the kids think *everything* of it. To them, grades are what school is about. The kids who are working hard are doing it more for the grades than for the "learning." The kids who aren't working have given up, because the grades they get never match the effort they put in . . . and an *F* tells them nothing about what they need to do to get better.

> They work to pass, not to know, and outraged science takes her revenge. They do pass and they don't know.
>
> —*Thomas Huxley*[1]

Grades are so meaningless. Say you've got a kid with a *C+* average. What does that mean? Does it mean he's a *D+* in science but a *B+* in history? Does it mean he's a really bad mathematician but a great writer? Does it mean he can't read, but pays attention and doesn't disrupt the class? It's wild to me. Then you have schools that say, "Ooh, now we'll get a little more specific." So they give a kid a 91 rather than an *A*. But it's the same thing. You take an English paper and you break it up mathematically, with 80 points for content, 10 points for grammar, 10 points for thesis statement . . . and that's how you get the number. It's all false. Even a *good* grade doesn't necessarily mean anything. Seymour Sarason puts it this way, "Now look, just because a child has a normal body temperature that doesn't mean he's not sick."

Grades are totally subjective, too. If the assignment was to build a ladder to the moon and a kid got halfway there, would you give her an *F* for lack of follow-through, or an *A* for perseverance and building a 120,000-mile ladder?

Alfie Kohn has done a great job demonstrating how grades have been scientifically proven to reduce students' interest in the learning itself, reduce students' preference for challenging tasks, and reduce the quality of students' thinking.[2] Despite all of this evidence, schools continue to emphasize the importance and validity of grading.

I remember one day, during the first year of The Met, when Lori stood up at her exhibition and told the audience that she had read one book that quarter. *One* book? Feeling a little embarrassed, I put my head down, and while it was down, I heard Lori say that it was the first book she had ever finished in her life. She was 15 years old.

It blew me away, because this was a kid who was getting *As* and *Bs* before she came to us. But she had never finished an entire book because she didn't have to. She got good grades regardless. If she needed to write a book report, she saw the movie or read the first and last chapters, and that was "enough." Lori put as much effort into the reading as her teachers did into evaluating her reading. They didn't see what she was missing, and she didn't tell them.

———◆———

I have been trying to get rid of grades my whole career. Unfortunately, in the United States, trying to get rid of grades is like trying to get us to embrace the metric system. People just don't want to change. You can hand a parent this long, beautiful, narrative description of their kid's progress and status, and they will turn around and say, "But how is he doing compared to the other kids?" or "But does he get an *A*?" That's how we've been programmed. At Thayer, my effort to do away with grades was met with so much resistance that I gave up the idea and went for a compromise instead. We kept grades, but added narratives as well. In fact, for parent-teacher conferences, I had the teachers discuss the child for a half hour *before* they pulled out the report card. In my experience, once a parent sees the letters on the report card, they stop listening. If their kid got an *A,* they're happy and they're ready to leave. If their kid got an *F,* they're pissed off at you and at the kid, and most aren't going to hear anything else.

We avoided all of this at The Met by deciding from the beginning that we wouldn't give grades. At the end of each quarter, every kid is evaluated through a one- to two-page narrative written by his or her advisor. Having a culture where narratives replace report card grades is in line with our philosophy of one student at a time. **To write a narrative, you've got to really look at the student.** It is easy to write down a single letter for a kid you barely know—but it tells that kid, and his parents, that you don't have any need or desire to get to know him better.

At The Met, we use narratives not to rank students or compare them to each other, but to help each student understand what he or she must do to meet his or her own learning goals and needs. In other words, when a teacher reads a student's paper, she is not reading it to mark the student's progress in relation to a predetermined set of activities and goals, but to actually figure out what those activities and goals *should be* for that student. When you say you want to get rid of grades, some people think you want to get rid of standards altogether. It's the exact opposite. Using narratives really forces schools to look more closely at each student's accomplishments and gaps. The standards are determined in a really personalized way by developing an individualized learning plan, with goals and indicators of achievement for each student. Then it's a matter of evaluating that student in a real-world way: **assessing the student's progress as it compares to what he or she will need in order to succeed in college and in life.** When you think about it, you can't hold students to any standard higher than that.

Yes, evaluating students through narratives is very hard to do. And it's very time-consuming. Narratives are hard because they force the teacher to understand a kid's life. He or she has to think about how to describe the way the kid gets along with adults, the kid's attitude toward learning, his work habits, and the gaps in skills and knowledge he needs to fill. Those are really hard things to describe. It's also true that when you're writing narratives every quarter, it can be tough to say something new about each kid every time. For example, you don't want to say for 16 narratives in a row that the kid's grown and she's got "a great attitude."

Narrative format is important here, because if it's designed right, it forces the teacher to go deeper: for example, to define growth and describe what he or she means by "a great attitude." Part of our Met narratives describes what the kid has actually done in terms of work, but the rest analyzes this work in terms of the school's learning goals (see Chapter 5, page 103), the teacher's individualized goals for the kid, the kid's goals for himself or herself, and the family's goals for the kid.

A kid might walk into the school and be a great speaker, but as that kid's teacher, you've got to be able to tell her how she can get even better. No narrative should be the same from quarter to quarter or from kid to kid. This is why "one student at a time" is so important. There might be a kid who enrolled in your school barely able to read, but who has worked his butt off and made great strides. If you compared him against one standard and used grades, you'd give him an *F*. But, if you compared him to himself and used a narrative, you'd be writing about where he's improved and giving him concrete guidance on how to improve more. Of course, parents should know that their high schooler is not yet ready to read a college-level text or that he is not yet able to do the kind of writing he'll need to do later in school and in life. A narrative is not meant to make every child look good, but to evaluate him or her realistically and through a broader lens.

The narrative is a tool to help learning. If the kid's really messing up and needs a reality check, then the narrative will be more critical. If you've been saying something over and over again in the classroom and the kid isn't hearing you, the narrative is where you put it in writing. And **the narrative is *not* evaluation for evaluation's sake.** It's evaluation with a purpose, and one of the challenges is making sure that it leads to something real. Maybe you need to tell the kid that he is lacking in certain areas; when you're writing the narrative, if you don't phrase this just right, you risk distancing the parents and decreasing the kid's motivation to learn more. So the question becomes, how do you write what is accurate, but also continue to push the learning?

Met advisors struggle with this question every quarter. Here is an example of an actual narrative, one that I think really demonstrates the right kind of balance between evaluation and motivation:

Excerpt from the Met narrative of a third-quarter 9th grader

Adjustment to the Met: During this past quarter, Michelle has adjusted to the rhythm of the Met week, which alternates between school and LTI. Though Michelle still struggles with the freedoms afforded her at The Met, I believe that she is making an effort to improve. She still needs to understand the meaning of the word "no" and understand that although The Met is a flexible place, there are certain things that are simply non-negotiable. She often gets frustrated and begins to get an attitude when she is told that she cannot do something precisely when she wants to do it. She needs to learn to think before asking for something—that is, she should begin to understand by herself what is reasonable and what is not. But, with all this said and done, it really should be noted that I have seen an incredible improvement in her behavior—her attitude is much better and she is making an effort to control her temper.

I want to mention here that, like Michelle's narrative, all of our 9th graders' narratives talk about their adjustment to The Met. With way too many kids in this country dropping out while still in their freshman year, this transition period from middle to high school is important in determining a kid's success in high school and beyond.[3] Even though everyone knows how important it is for a kid to adjust to the high school learning environment, do you see "adjustment" on any traditional school report cards? No. You also rarely see report cards that talk about the kid's personal growth. Or about her time management skills. Or about whether or not she is becoming an independent learner. These are all real-world things that we deem extremely important in employees. Don't most employees get write-ups or evaluations with comments like, "She doesn't hand things in on time" or "She works well in a team"? These are the same things that we look at in our kids at The Met. And we try to give them the same kind of feedback they would get in the real world.

Another example:

Excerpt from the Met narrative of a third-quarter 10th grader

Overview: Barry is an absolute pleasure to have in the advisory. He is still a stabilizing force—respected, respectful, and never complaining. Watching his growth this year has been amazing. . . . He is easygoing and so easy to work with. As a result of his success at his internship, his confidence has grown—not only as a student, but also in his ability to admit to problems that he is having with work. He no longer tries to find excuses, which is really wonderful to see. If Barry just continues to make progress as he has been making, he will keep tapping his great potential and his results will be astounding. It's an exciting thought.

Of course, the narratives also focus on the student's development of specific essential skills. We note and follow their progress in areas like mathematics, computer programs (PowerPoint, Excel, and so forth), and research skills. We also assess skills relevant to the student's internship:

Excerpt from the Met narrative of a fourth-quarter 10th grader

Overview: Toby's fourth-quarter project was a continuation of her third-quarter project: establish and maintain a school aquarium, then teach a team of people proper maintenance and the scientific reasons behind the maintenance. She created a list of research-framing questions, set out a timetable for research, and bought pH paper to test common substances around the house, but did not follow through on her experiment or her reading for investigation. She has a basic understanding of pH, but, as yet, it is not connected to her project work.

So there's a little sample of what narratives written by people who really know the students can say both *about* those kids and *to* those kids, their parents, and anyone else who reads them. The alternative approach, of course, is to have teachers sit at home at the end of the quarter and add up meaningless numbers to come up with meaningless letters. That is so sad to me. And such a waste of a teacher's talent and energy.

———◆———

One final note on grades. I realize we may never get rid of them completely. I'm not advocating a system that cannot adapt to the demands of a world that continues to view grades as a valid form of student evaluation and continues to require them for things like college admission and scholarships. At the end of every year, Met staff spend time converting our juniors' and seniors' narratives into the grade point averages they need to apply to particular colleges or for certain scholarships. This involves looking carefully at the narratives and translating them into categories that grade-focused institutions feel comfortable with.

If you're thinking that this process is too subjective, it is, but as I've been saying, so are grades! If a kid needs a transcript full of letter grades to get into college, we look carefully at the narrative records of his performance and figure out which grades would be appropriate. Or if a kid comes to us saying she can get 10 percent off her car insurance if she has a *B* average, we don't argue with the insurance companies about the value of grades. We look at her narratives, and if we believe they would translate into a *B* average, that is what we show the insurance company. We do what's right for our kids day to day by giving narratives instead of grades, but we aren't stupid about the way the world unfortunately works. We do not want to deny Met students any opportunities that will positively influence their futures.

Tests vs. Exhibitions

> [In] the traditional method the child must say something that he has merely learned. There is all the difference in the world between having something to say, and having to say something.
>
> ~ *John Dewey*

I don't need to say anything new here about why it's more valuable for kids to stand up and show what they've learned than it is for them to fill in bubbles on a standardized test. Even the people who are fighting so hard for standards-based reform will admit that public exhibitions can give both teachers and parents a good understanding of what a kid knows, or at least what the kid has accomplished up to that point. In 1984, Ted Sizer picked up where John Dewey left off and made diploma by exhibition (rather than by grades or by seat time) one of the core principles of the Coalition of Essential Schools. And most schools today totally agree with Ted. But that's the theory winning, not the practice.

It's sad, but most of the schools that want to use exhibitions don't, simply because of the scheduling nightmare. Yes, I agree that within the traditional 45-minutes-per-class school schedule it is really hard to find time for 2,000 kids to demonstrate what they've learned in front of their teachers, peers, and families. Smaller schools and nontraditional scheduling is the obvious answer here. Again, we need to bust things up; otherwise, we are just tweaking around the edges.

On a deeper level, those of us who believe in exhibitions need to be clearer about their true purpose. Exhibitions have to be used to promote growth, not to sort students in the same way test scores do. **Exhibitions have to be conversations about learning** between the students and their teachers, peers, and families.

Exhibitions, and all the work that goes before and after them, emphasize **the process of learning,** not just the end product. At The Met, advisors are constantly asking students to talk about the process they used to get to where they are, to show drafts of the final papers they're presenting, to think about what needs to come next. And, although exhibitions are set up to assess what has happened in the previous weeks, they must also include goal setting for future growth. They must be part of a continuous and connected cycle of learning.

During The Met's first year, one of our freshmen, Tricia, did an exhibition that was a beautiful example of what an exhibition should be. It was like a dress rehearsal for her as she was beginning **to learn how to talk about her learning.** Tricia had her portfolio of work laid out; she had drafts of a story she was writing, showing her progress; she had excerpts of a book she was reading; she had examples from her algebra workshop; she had a learning plan she'd developed with her advisor and her mother; and she had a five-page paper that explained how all her learning over the quarter met the goals she'd set for herself. During her presentation, Tricia talked in depth about the book she was reading and had her audience reading along and learning about symbolism. It was a formative and beautiful assessment of the work she had done to that point. This exhibition laid the groundwork that Tricia's advisor used over the next 10 weeks to help Tricia meet her learning goals.

Here was a 9th grader talking about her learning in a way you won't see many other 9th graders talking. Here was an exhibition, like so many others I've seen, that made the whole question of whether tests or exhibitions are better for assessing students totally beside the point. If you were Tricia's parent, after seeing all this **real evidence of her learning,** you would *never* be satisfied with a simple test score again. Six years later, this kid (who is now an adult) is still looking at her learning as something she owns and still setting her own high standards. And she is making some great choices.

Of course, I could also give you plenty of examples of bad exhibitions—exhibitions where students stumbled through their

. . . Wednesday morning I just started to cry. My experiences with the exhibitions were so good, I couldn't contain myself. I was so moved by the seriousness of the students, the proud parents and advisors. The looks on the students' faces as they nervously started, and the looks as they finished; the deep breaths, the hugs and the satisfaction . . .

presentations, didn't show any evidence of work they'd done, and couldn't answer the panel's questions. **But even in these worst-case scenarios, the exhibition is a learning tool, because it allows the kid to really see what he or she doesn't know.** Even the worst exhibitions end up teaching students about the importance of preparation and planning, helping them build their public speaking skills, and giving them a clear picture of what they'll need to work on before their next exhibition. I have seen many students totally pumped up after a terrible exhibition. Doing poorly actually increases their motivation. Rarely does a student who fails a test walk away from it with a new understanding of what she doesn't know and excited about learning more so she can do better next time. With tests, there usually isn't a next time, anyway.

———◆———

Schools that use exhibitions as a method of assessment need to make sure that the students, staff, and parents understand the requirements and purpose of exhibitions. They also need to maximize exhibitions' incredible value in building relationships in the school.

First, exhibitions are an amazing opportunity for parent involvement. Parents get to see their kids in action and get to actually hear them talk about what they've done and what they've learned, rather than just guessing about it based on a report card grade or assuming it's happened because the kids are walking across the stage at graduation. An exhibition is a chance for every parent to see his or her child perform, a chance to be proud. It is also a chance for them to question their child about school and not have him say, "It's fine," and then walk away and go to his room. Our Met parents say things like, "I loved seeing my son's autobiography—I was so proud to see how he'd written more than 100 pages analyzing his life and his education," and "I was amazed to watch my daughter take her love for marine biology and develop her own curriculum so she could teach it to the other kids at her school."

Second, exhibitions are a great opportunity for teachers to really work together as a team. By sitting in on exhibitions given by their colleagues' students, individual teachers become part of a community that is invested in helping to teach each child. This opportunity to witness another teacher's struggles or successes with individual students also helps all teachers become better equipped to provide the kind of collegial support that is vital to a healthy school.

Third, exhibitions are an opportunity to include the outside community in education by inviting others to come in and watch: local leaders, college students, professors, mentors, school board members, everyone. Every time I watch exhibitions at The Met, I'm reminded that I'm seeing our most sophisticated student-adult conversations. The interaction between the student and the audience creates a whole new level of communication where the student is at the center but is also receiving input from everyone about his or her learning.

Fourth, exhibitions promote rather than inhibit growth. This means that when an exhibition isn't that great, or when the kid really isn't prepared or hasn't shown progress on his work, it is still an opportunity for others to see and applaud growth in other areas. In situations where I don't feel students did a great job on their exhibitions, I have to remember to ask myself, "Not great *compared to what?*" Even after a "bad" exhibition, I have heard parents say things like, "My son has *never* talked like that in front of a group before—I can't believe he did that!" One of our students started her exhibition by warning the audience that she had a stutter. As it turned out, she didn't stutter once during the entire presentation—but if she had, she would have been showing us her courage, her determination to keep going and to make herself understood. With every exhibition, there is always an upside, always something learned. When you fail a test, you just fail, end of story. There is no end to the story with exhibitions. The learning keeps on happening.

Fifth, exhibitions completely eliminate cheating. In a 1998 survey by *Who's Who Among American High School Students,* 80 percent of college-bound high schoolers admitted they'd cheated at least once.[4] As a Met student once said, "You can cheat your way through other high schools and you can cheat your way through elementary and middle school, but here you cannot cheat at all. It's impossible. When you have to stand in front of everyone and do your exhibition, you've got to have something."[5]

Sixth, exhibitions encourage students to go deeper with their learning by requiring them to create and present a portfolio of their work. Where studying for a test may involve students looking at class notes and rereading textbooks, preparing a portfolio requires students to look at and define the many layers of their learning. This can mean sharing successive drafts of a paper, showing photos of a project in various phases of construction, and all sorts of other things. Deep learning is so important, and such a thrill to do and to watch.

Tests can do a lot of damage to a person who really wants to take learning further, branch out, learn more. I saw it myself back in college. My roommate and I were taking the same English course and had to read Joseph Conrad's *Heart of Darkness.* I read the book eight times (and ended up hating it) because it was going to be on the test and I knew I had to "know" it. My roommate loved the book and went on to read every book Conrad had ever written. I got an *A* on the test. My roommate got a *D.*

Clearly, deeper learning was not valued in that course. I got the "good" grade, but I knew my roommate had learned more than I had and that he had gotten more out of the book. And I envied the way he pursued his passion.

Finally, exhibitions allow, and require, students to set high standards for themselves. When they don't do well at an exhibition, they know it—immediately. They don't have to wait for a test score to come back to tell them they need to work harder. And if they have a personalized learning plan (like all Met students do), *they* help determine what constitutes "doing well." Exhibitions force students to become accountable for and take control of their own learning. Isn't that what we're striving for?

Questions to Further This Conversation . . .

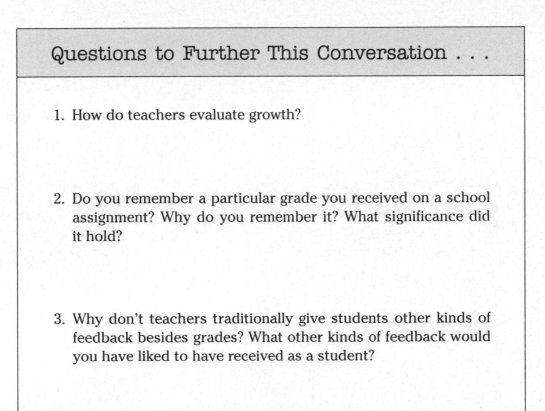

1. How do teachers evaluate growth?

2. Do you remember a particular grade you received on a school assignment? Why do you remember it? What significance did it hold?

3. Why don't teachers traditionally give students other kinds of feedback besides grades? What other kinds of feedback would you have liked to have received as a student?

4. Dewey writes, "[In] the traditional method the child must say something that he has merely learned. There is all the difference in the world between having something to say, and having to say something."[6] What does this quote mean to you?

5. Make the argument that grades are objective. Now make the counterargument that grades are subjective. Which argument fits best with your other beliefs about learning and education?

"Nobody grew taller by being measured."

~ Phillip Gammage

Chapter 8½

Standards and How Testing Has Nothing to Do with Them

It's test time! The following essay questions are intended to assess whether you truly understand how ridiculous standardized tests are and how they have nothing to do with the standards we actually want our students to achieve.

1. What if we measured students "one student at a time"?

2. What if we assessed students' learning by measuring whether it made them want to learn more?

3. What if we evaluated students in a way that motivated them to work harder?

4. What if the "high stakes" were stakes that were applicable to real life?

5. What if we could give all students individualized tests that showed how much they had learned in comparison with what they knew before and the process they used to get there?

6. What if the people who really know and care about individual students were allowed to set the standards for them, instead of leaving it to someone in the government or at a big publishing company to decide what every student should know?

7. What if we held our students to the same standards the world will hold them to when they get out of school?

8. What if we thought about standards not as external things that students must measure up to in a test they get once every few months or years, but as things they internalize and hold themselves to every day?

9. What if we evaluated students' performance through real performance assessments, where they exhibit their work to people who care about them and their learning?

10. What if I (and my colleagues) could stop feeling so angry about standardization and standardized tests? Yeah, what if!

——————◆——————

Kenneth Wesson, a founding member of the Association of Black Psychologists, once said, brilliantly, "Let's be honest. If poor, inner-city children consistently outscored children from wealthy suburban homes on standardized tests, is anyone naive enough to believe we would still insist on using these tests as indicators of success?"[1] Yes, come on, let's be honest. The answer is no.

There is no one indicator of success that fits every kid. There can be no one set of standards for every student in the country. There will never be one test that measures what every kid knows. Former U.S. Secretary of Labor Robert B. Reich said it perfectly when he pointed out the paradox of stressing standardized tests when everyone agrees that standardized jobs are on the way out. "There's one certainty about what today's high school students will be doing a decade from now," Reich wrote. "They won't all be doing the same things, and they won't be drawing on the same body of knowledge."[2] As Reich also explained, "We're creating a one-size fits all system that needlessly brands many young people as failures when they might thrive if offered a different education whose progress was measured differently."[3]

In private conversations, many teachers have told me they can more accurately assess their students through their day-to-day interactions than through standardized tests. But because most of us are not against quantitative data *in principle,* we stick to the measurement methods we are given and that are demanded of us. What we should be doing is spending our energy (not to mention all the money that's gone into developing these tests) to **find real ways to measure what makes good schools and successful students.**

In Rhode Island, we have a commissioner of education, Peter McWalters, who was wise enough to know that in order to evaluate and understand the success of the state's schools he needed more than just reading and math scores. So he helped implement a completely different kind of measurement tool called the SALT survey (short for "School Accountability for Learning and Teaching"), which looks at the things that are really important and surveys students, parents, *and* staff. Here are my favorite questions from the SALT survey:

Students

❋ How often do you talk to a teacher about school-related problems?
❋ How often do you talk to a teacher about personal problems?

Parents

❋ Do you agree that the school views parents as important partners?
❋ Do you agree that this school is a safe place?

Teachers

❋ How often do students receive individual mentoring and coaching?
❋ How often do students engage in real-world learning activities?
❋ Please indicate the extent to which you agree or disagree that the following phrase describes your job: "Participation in decision making."

These aren't my favorite questions just because The Met scores off the charts on them compared to other schools in the state (although I am quite proud of that). They are my favorites because they get at what is truly important but hardly ever measured.

What scares me so much and makes me so angry is that in all this talk about standardized tests and consequences for "low-performing" schools, nobody is measuring whether schools are developing **healthy human beings.** Ask people what they want for their children, and they will answer that they want them to be happy, to show a love of learning, to be respectful, to be kind, to have real skills, to make a contribution to the world. Then look at what schools teach and how they test it. The tests are way off the mark.

Another thing that makes me angry is how totally backward it is to reward a school or a teacher whose kids get higher scores by increasing that school's or teacher's funding. If the government really thinks that meeting the state- or federally-determined standards is important, then it should be putting its money where its priorities are by giving more funding to the schools that are having trouble meeting the standards!

Forget about leaving no child behind; we are not only leaving kids behind, but destroying them in the process. As Robert J. Sternberg has pointed out, "Once students get low scores on aptitude tests . . . they come to think of themselves as dumb. Even if they achieve, they may view themselves as achieving in spite of their being dumb. Society may view them in the same way."[4]

As I'm writing this, Texas is leading the country in the current high-stakes testing experiment. But look closer at how much Texas's dropout rates have increased since they've implemented the program. "In fact, 7 of the 20 urban districts in the nation with the worst dropout rates are now located in Texas. Nationally, 9 of the 10 states with the highest dropout rates have graduation tests, whereas none of the 10 states with the highest graduation rates have such a policy.[5] You tell a kid who failed the state test last year that he has to take it again this year, and he's gonna say, "Why bother?" and drop out.

The following is an excerpt from a July 18, 2002, article in *The Boston Globe*. The emphases are mine.

Schools: Many Who Failed MCAS Quit

July 18, 2002 BOSTON

Boston school officials announced findings yesterday that **a significant number** of the students in the Class of 2003 who failed the high-stakes MCAS exam in the spring of 2001 and who did not take the retest in December of 2001 **have dropped out of high school.**

Data released at yesterday's School Committee meeting showed that of the 1,675 students who failed the math portion of the Massachusetts Comprehensive Assessment System exam in the spring, 572 students did not take the retest. Of the 572, 168 dropped out of high school.

Remaining in school were 278 who simply did not take the test again. Transfers out of the system accounted for 106 and the other 20 withdrew because they were expelled, hospitalized, or in jail.

On the English portion of the test, 1,330 students did not pass the first exam, and 379 did not take the retest. Of the 379, 107 dropped out. Of the remaining students, 187 didn't take the exam, 68 transferred out of the district, and 17 withdrew because they were expelled, hospitalized, or in jail.

School officials could not say how much overlap there is in the data between the two portions of the exam.

So far, **51 percent of the Class of 2003 in Boston have yet to pass the exam.**

School Committee chairwoman Elizabeth Reilinger said **she is concerned about the high number of students who remained in school but did not take the retest.**

"Something is wrong with this picture," she said. "I don't know where the disconnect is and I am trying to get a sense of that."

She is concerned about the kids who haven't taken the retest? What about the kids who dropped out? What about the ones who were expelled, hospitalized, or sent to jail? It frightens me that our priorities can get so out of whack when it comes to testing.

It also frightens me that so many educators, parents, and kids don't know how these tests are made and how flawed the thinking behind them is. First, it is important to understand that there are currently five widely used standardized achievement tests distributed throughout the United States. Some states may promote the fact that they use a standards-based test that is in line with their state's own curricular goals. What they don't tell you is that most of these state-customized tests are built by one of the five companies that design the national tests. As W. James Popham explains in *The Truth About Testing,* "Consequently, many of the criticisms that can be leveled at the national tests can also be aimed quite accurately at statewide standardized achievement tests."[6]

In this book, Popham dissects standardized achievement tests and defines three powerful reasons why **these tests should not be used to determine the effectiveness of a school's or a teacher's instructional practices.** First, as with everything in education, there is no "one-size-fits-all" test. "If you look carefully at what the items in a standardized achievement test are actually measuring," Popham writes, "you'll often find that *half or more of what's tested wasn't even supposed to be taught* in a particular district or state."[7] Second, due to test developers' search for reliability, the items that a majority of students are most likely to do well on are removed from the tests. This means that **test makers eliminate the exact content that teachers have emphasized and students have mastered.** Finally, Popham dedicates an entire chapter to the notion that these tests "should not be used to judge the quality of students' schooling because factors other than instruction also influence students' performance on these tests" (e.g., curriculum content, socioeconomic status, and inherited academic aptitudes).[8]

Please read some of the articles and books listed in the next section. They say just about everything that needs to be said about the horrors and total failings of standardized testing and national standards.

Some Great Resources on Standards and Standardized Testing

Berger, Ron. (1997). *Building a School Culture of High Standards*. Available: http://www.newhorizons.org/strategies/arts/cabc/berger.htm.

Bracey, Gerald. (5 December 2000). *High Stakes Testing*. Available: http://www.asu.edu/educ/epsl/EPRU/documents/cerai-00-32.htm.

Bracey, Gerald. (2002). *Put to the Test: An Educator's and Consumer's Guide to Standardized Testing*. Bloomington, IN: Phi Delta Kappa International.

FairTest: The National Center for Fair and Open Testing [Web site]. Available: http://www.fairtest.org.

Kohn, Alfie. (2000). *The Case Against Standardized Testing: Raising the Scores, Ruining the Schools*. Portsmouth, NH: Heinemann.

Kohn, Alfie. (2001). *Fighting the Tests: A Practical Guide to Rescuing Our Schools*. Available: http://www.alfiekohn.org/teaching/ftt.htm.

Lemann, Nicholas. (1999). *The Big Test: The Secret History of the American Meritocracy*. New York: Farrar, Straus & Giroux.

Levine, Mel. (2002). *A Mind at a Time*. New York: Simon & Schuster.

Meier, Deborah. (2000). *In Schools We Trust: Creating Communities of Learning in an Era of Testing and Standardization*. Boston: Beacon Press.

Meier, Deborah. (2000). *Will Standards Save Public Education? A New Democracy Forum with Deborah Meier, edited by Joshua Cohen and Joel Rogers for the Boston Review*. Boston: Beacon Press.

Ohanian, Susan. (1999). *One Size Fits Few.* Portsmouth, NH: Heinemann.

Owen, David. (1999). "The Cult of Mental Measurement." In David Owen and Marilyn Doerr (Eds.), *None of the Above: The Truth Behind the SATs* (pp. 173–191). Lanham, MD: Rowman & Littlefield.

Popham, W. James. (2001). *The Truth About Testing: An Educator's Call to Action.* Alexandria, VA: Association for Supervision and Curriculum Development.

Reich, Robert B. (11 July 2000). "One Education Does Not Fit All." *The American Prospect Online.* Available: http://www.prospect.org/web features/2000/07/reich-r-07-11.html.

Reich, Robert B. (20 June 2001). "Standards for What?" *Education Week 20*(41): 64, 48.

Sarason, Seymour. (1993). *Letters to a Serious Education President.* Newbury Park, CA: Corwin Press. (See page 59, especially.)

Seuss, Dr., with Jack Prelutsky and Lane Smith. (1999). *Hooray for Diffendoofer Day!* New York: Alfred A. Knopf.

Steele, Claude M. (August 1999). "Thin Ice: 'Stereotype Threat' and Black College Students." *The Atlantic Monthly, 284*(2): 44–54. Available: http://www.theatlantic.com/issues/99aug/9908stereotype.htm.

Wesson, Kenneth A. (22 November 2002). "The 'Volvo' Effect." *Education Week, 20*(12): 34–36.

White, N. (1 October 2001). "Project-Based Learning and High Standards at Shutesbury Elementary." *Edutopia Online.* Available: http://www.glef.org/php/article.php?id=Art182.

Wolk, Ronald A. (April 2002). "Multiple Measures." *Teacher Magazine, 13*(7): 3.

Closing Thoughts

I want to end this mini-chapter with an incredible essay by one of our Met students, written (oddly enough) for the state writing test. The prompt asked students to write a letter to the Board of Education regarding a proposal to implement a new high-stakes exam.

> Dear Chairperson:
>
> I really personally disagree with the proposal. First, I want to tell you that everyone in this school has a different level of learning. It won't be fair that just because they don't pass a test, they can't stay in school. Everyone deserves a chance.
>
> For example: Let's say that you are just learning how to ride a bike and you keep falling. You decide to try one more time, but this time, you don't fall. You're proud of yourself, right? What if someone says that because you fell the first time, they have to take your bike away? They are not giving you a chance to prove to them that you can ride a bike.
>
> Just think about it. If students don't graduate, they don't go to college and don't become what they want to be. I'm sure that nobody ever stopped you from being what you are now. Just because a person is blind doesn't mean that they don't have vision, and just because a person can't walk doesn't mean they can't travel a distance. Well, just because a person doesn't pass a test doesn't mean that they are not good enough to go on. If you give them a chance, all the chances that they need, I'm more than sure that in the future, they'll succeed.
>
> Everyone deserves a chance in life, and nobody has the right to take it away from them. Everyone learns from their mistakes. If they don't learn the first time, they'll probably learn the second time. It's really up to them.
>
> Sincerely,
> Vanessa Cuevas
> Met Student

Pretty eloquent for a kid, huh? I like writing tests the best because they actually do what you want a test to do—show what each kid knows by letting him or her demonstrate it in an individual way. But I don't like them because they ask every kid the exact same question. What if the kid isn't interested in that particular subject? If you ask one kid a question on a subject he's really passionate about, you're going to get some good writing. If you ask another kid, you might get writing that looks nothing like what she is really capable of producing, and you might get nothing at all. The year Vanessa wrote this, we were very lucky because first, there was an actual writing portion of the state test and second, the prompt was something that nearly all our kids were passionate about . . . disagreeing with!

Another year, the Rhode Island state test writing question asked kids to write about freedom of speech in school newspapers. One of our students responded by pointing out that the question was not appropriate for kids like him who go to small schools that don't have school newspapers. He probably didn't score very well. In my book, he scored off the charts just on his ability to reason and express his (unconventional) thoughts on paper. Then there was the time that a student told me she had chosen not to respond to the state test's prompt because she had no opinion on the subject and couldn't come up with anything in the allotted time. Instead, she wrote an essay about why she hates standardized tests!

We've got to change the way we assess kids and the standards we hold them to. There is no one standard, there is no one test, and there is no one set of questions that is going to tell you what you want to know about how individual students are doing in a particular school. To the district or state or nation, the kids who take standardized tests are numbers used to set policies and distribute funding. To Vanessa, they are her friends and classmates, who want and need to be evaluated as individuals. And we all agree with her, right?

Questions to Further This Conversation . . .

1. What effect does testing have on learning?

2. What effect does testing have on the learning that comes after the test?

3. What do you remember about the tests you've taken in your life?

4. Tell about a time when you were aware that your knowledge and potential—or a student's—was misrepresented by a standardized test.

5. Think about something that you know well enough to teach to others. What would be the best way to measure how well they've learned it?

"You must be the change you wish to see in the world."

~ Mahatma Gandhi

Chapter **9**

Make It Happen

Gandhi's quote about being the change you wish to see in the world, along with Tom Peters's quietly profound statement, **"Problems are my friends,"** have been the mantras that have gotten me through many a day. Anyone in schools knows how important mantras can be to calm the soul and reenergize the will to go on.

When Tom studied the most successful businesses in the world, he noted that the ones that make it are the ones that say, "A problem? All right, let's go after it." This is what we need to be saying every day in our schools. This perseverance is what will make a school strong, what will make it different. There is no time to complain; we have a job to do. We have kids to help.

None of us are in the schools because we want it easy. **If we wanted it easy, we'd be doing another job.** And so we can't get freaked out by the problems all the time. We may never solve all the problems we face, but we have to be able to get excited about the fact that we at least have the opportunity to do something about these problems . . . that we are in the place where the changes we are making really can be the changes we wish to see in the world.

Change is not only possible, it is necessary. We are losing our children and they are losing their futures.

> The world will not evolve past its current state of crisis by using the same thinking that created the situation.
>
> *~ Albert Einstein*

———◆———

Everything I have said here in this book is about more than creating better schools. It is about saving our children. And it is about justice. In 1961, Myles Horton turned over the Citizenship Schools program to Martin Luther King Jr. and the Southern Christian Leadership Conference (SCLC). The Citizenship Schools, part of Horton's Highlander education program, were set up to educate activists and catalyze social change with what Horton called a "two-eye" theory of teaching—keeping one eye on where people are and one eye on where they can be.[1] When Highlander turned the program over to the SCLC, Horton gave a speech that included the following words—words that I think apply equally to the struggle for a better system of education:

> I want the struggle for social and economic justice to get big and become so dynamic that the atmosphere in which you're working is so charged that sparks are darting around very fast, and they explode and create other sparks, and it's almost perpetual motion. Learning jumps from person to person with no visible explanation of how it happened.[2]

It is time to change the strategies. It is time to undo the self-fulfilling prophecies of too many principals and teachers who say that nothing can be done, that none of us is strong enough, or that this is the way it must be because this is the way it's always been. It is time to change the system of education. And if need be, we'll do it one school at a time.

Change

I'm not a huge car enthusiast, but I sometimes find great nuggets about innovation and change in the auto section of the local paper. One of the best things I've read appeared in a March 2002 *Providence Journal* article, which quoted GM Chief Executive Rick Wagoner saying about their new cars, "We started with the premise, 'What if we were inventing the automobile today rather than a century ago? What might we do differently?'" It is a powerful question to ask ourselves as we set out to design and open new schools. As Dee Hock, founder of Visa, often says, "The problem is never how to get new, innovative thoughts into your mind, but how to get the old ones out."

When it comes to education, we not only have trouble thinking outside the box, we put ourselves so far inside the box that we can't even *see* what's outside. I remember during the second year of The Met, a bunch of us were discussing changing something, and someone said, "But we have always done it this way." Everyone just stopped and laughed, because "always" was just one year and we had really only done "it" once. But already "it" was hard to change.

A school has to be a living organism. It has to be changing all the time and be ready to change at any moment. A great school is like a successful business in that it keeps looking at itself, questioning its operations, and making adjustments accordingly: when the kids change, when technology changes, when priorities change, when new research findings suggest a better way. There can't be one specific curriculum;

every student needs to have his or her own curriculum. Our curriculum at The Met—our "particular way of ordering content and purposes for teaching and learning"[3]—is simply **whatever is best for each kid.**

At The Met, we make small changes every day. Every kid's learning plan gets changed when the kid discovers a new interest, or when the teacher realizes the kid needs to become a better reader before he or she can pursue other goals. Contrast this with a traditional school, where a student might fail the same grade three times, and each year come back to the exact same curriculum. Nothing changes.

Some more examples from The Met: We once changed the entire daily schedule in the middle of the year to accommodate a teacher's idea that we "buddy" older students with younger students and set aside time for them to meet and work together. We've reworked the format of our transcript over and over to meet the demands of the colleges our students want to attend. We've recruited students through local Asian newspapers and churches after noticing an imbalance in the diversity of our student body. I am very proud of how often we have shifted or completely revamped our way of doing things (while always staying true to our underlying philosophy) because it demonstrates our **constant attention to the needs of our community and a commitment to filling those needs.**

———————◆———————

We are now at a point where we must educate our children in what no one knew yesterday, and prepare our schools for what no one knows yet.

~ *Margaret Mead*

Most schools need drastic change. I believe there is only so much change we can bring about within the present, confining, 45-minute-period, subject-oriented school. To truly meet kids' needs, there must be a major paradigm shift. Educators who are set in their ways must get "unset," must open their eyes and minds. And **all of us must constantly question what we are doing.** The only rhythm to get into is the rhythm of change.

It may sound antithetical, but it *is* possible to set up strong structures that promote flexible change. One of these structures is the habit of reflection, which is a huge part of the way we do things at The Met. As a school community, we're always thinking about what we're doing and our successes or struggles—writing in journals, having long group and one-on-one discussions, and writing our weekly staff TGIF newsletter. Another structure that we have created at The Met is a longitudinal study that will allow us to follow our kids from year to year, up to and beyond graduation. It is one systematic way of looking at what we're doing and getting the kind of feedback we can use to make real changes.

The philosophy that I've been discussing in this book is similar to the philosophy that I had when I applied for my first principalship in 1972, which is similar to the philosophy of The Met. But The Met looks very different from my first school because it is a different time, with different kids and different teachers. I'm different, too. My philosophy is also pretty similar to the one John Dewey had many years before I was born—but again, his lab school looked very different from The Met. Finally, I know that what we are doing now at The Met may not work in 2 years, 5 years, 10 years. But I also know that if we, as a school community, respect and trust one another and rely on our collective spirit and intelligence, we can find an approach that will work. We keep asking ourselves questions about learning, structures, assessments, curriculum, and teacher roles. We stick to our philosophy, pay attention to what the latest research is saying, and keep changing the paths we use to carry out our philosophy according to the times, the kids, and the staff. Maybe the most symbolic expression of this is that when we set out to build the four new Met schools in Providence, we chose a design that included moveable walls. Even the physical structure of a school must be able to change with the times and the needs of the people inside it.

This constant readiness to change does not frustrate me or make me uncomfortable, as it often does others. It makes me excited that I always have a chance to find new ways to do my job. It is very exciting to be learning every day **how to educate our children better.** It will always be a struggle, but to me, it's an exciting struggle. One of my colleagues, Elaine Hackney, once offered the following sage words: **"Don't confuse discomfort for not being successful."**

After I started at Thayer, I wrote a chapter for a book in which I said something that I can say now about The Met and the new schools that The Big Picture Company is starting around the country:

> What will it look like when the school has been functioning for years? Unfortunately, I don't exactly know, but that is what is exciting. That is what is beautiful about turning theory into practice. That is what is invigorating about solving a problem.[4]

Or as Sir Francis Bacon once said, "If a man will begin with certainties, he shall end in doubts; but if he will be content to begin with doubts he shall end in certainties."

It is easy to understand why many teachers revert to textbooks or worksheets when things around them are in constant, challenging motion, but they must learn to be in motion, too. The kids are being loud; they are having a hard time paying attention to each other; they are having a hard time paying attention to the teacher. We all know that telling students to turn to page 37 and answer the questions can relieve chaos and make the room quieter for a time. I've recently heard of a new trend of teachers using wireless microphones in an effort to keep students' attention and be heard above the other noise in the classroom. Education is not about who can speak the loudest. It's about the students and teacher *wanting* to listen to each other. A truly personalized, small school allows that to happen.

Another reason I look to my friend Tom Peters for ideas on how to deal with the tough moments is because he titled one of his books *Thriving on Chaos*.[5] Tom told me it took him a long time to land on that word "thriving." But he was looking for a way of saying you must be ready for and enjoy the process of change. Our schools must be thriving environments, thriving on the chaos and on the beauty.

Leaders in every industry have used some version of the famous Wayne Gretzky quote, "I don't skate to where the puck is; I skate to where the puck is going to be," to inspire their people to look to where they want to be, rather than at where they are. The line may be overused, and some say that Gretzky never even said it, but I still think it's a great metaphor for what we, as educators, must do every day: look at our students now and imagine what they will need when they get to where they are going. In fact, for our purposes, we could change the quote to "skate to where the student is *and* to where they are going to be." **We all need to reexamine our situations from time to time and make sure we are not sticking to old patterns in new situations.**

People often talk to me about the great advantages I've had in being able to start schools from scratch—first at Shoreham and then at The Met. I agree that this is a huge bonus, mostly because starting fresh lets the administrator choose the staff—undoubtedly the most important choice an administrator makes.

But once a new school starts, it has the same dilemma that all schools have: How do you change things that you don't feel are right and, at the same time, take care of the kids in front of you every hour? **It is like trying to change a tire while the car is still moving.** At The Met, we take a lot of time to meet as a staff, away from the students—more time than in any school I have ever known. We have a monthly retreat day, weekly staff meetings, monthly grade-team meetings, and more . . . but it is still so hard.

It is also hard to change because all of us are working so earnestly, and it can be painful to look at our weaknesses. The key is to find the balance. To feel good about what we are doing, yet comfortable enough to critique our work and move forward. Although it sounds stupid to some, I like to say that **our work *is* our work.** Everything we do as educators— what we read, what we write, what we say to our students, what we say to each other—*is* our work.

I can hear people saying, "But there are only so many hours in the day," and "What about bus schedules and lunch duty?" Life is about priorities. So you make your philosophy the priority. At The Met, everything we do comes back to "one kid at a time." We've still got busing issues and lunches, but we try to set up a "good enough" structure for all of it that supports our ability to run our school and lets us focus primarily on our philosophy. We check everything against our mantras of one student at a time, real work, learning through interests, and family engagement.

What does that really mean? Well, it means that we do some things not so well so that we can do the more important stuff better. It's as simple as that. Every principal and teacher has to deal with paperwork, but it's up to them to choose which paperwork is a priority. **Your priorities will be clear to everyone who walks into your school or your classroom.** Your priorities will *really* be clear when someone walks up to one of your students, now or 10 years from now, and asks them about their experience at your school. If you are their teacher or principal, what do you hope they will say?

———◄●►———

The best thing about a school that can "change on a dime" and a school culture that is built on the idea of one kid at a time is that when something happens—a crisis, say—it's not treated as this separate thing to deal with before you get back to what you "really should be doing": the books everyone is reading or the specific content set out in the day's lesson plans. The crisis becomes the content. It becomes what the students' learning and the staff's jobs are about at that moment.

At Thayer, there was a girl whose father was molesting her. And she finally admitted it, went to her mom, and went to the police. The day of the trial came, and the girl went down to the courthouse, testified, and came back to school. I put aside what I was doing and spent some time talking to her. Then I told her to go to her algebra class. I remember that moment vividly, and I remember knowing that she didn't belong in an algebra class right then, that algebra had absolutely nothing to do with what her life was about at that moment. But I had no place else to send her. The school was not set up to support her in the way she needed. Or to support me, as I tried to help her.

Compare this to the way The Met was able to respond when one of our students was randomly shot and killed in front of his home. The next morning, no one was worrying about the tests they'd have to postpone or deciding if they should cancel a field trip. No bells were ringing telling the students to stop crying, move on, go to algebra. Everything we were already planning to do that day fit with what we had to do to come together as a community and get through that terrible time. Because everything we had to do that day was about being there for our students, about meeting their needs, about serving as a safe environment for them and their families, about creating a culture of respect and caring. Mourning our student *was* the curriculum.

Friends of Change

When Robby Fried and I came up with the dirty dozen list of the "enemies of change" (see Chapter 2, pages 36–37), we also came up with a half dozen "friends of change." Whether you are a teacher, an administrator, a parent, a student, or a community member, if you are willing to proceed despite the obstacles, these are a few concepts that will help you keep the wheels of change in motion:

1. *Concentration:* Figure out what you stand for and try to make it a part of everything you do regarding the school. Put your philosophy up on the wall, if that's what it takes to keep it in focus. Explain to people why you're dissatisfied with "business as usual." Don't let the conflicting demands and multiple distractions of day-to-day school affairs make you stray from your vision.

2. *Commitment:* Change doesn't happen easily or quickly. Educational fads and slogans come and go; people stay. Commitment to serious school change means commitment to *being there*. If the dreams are the right ones, they're worth holding onto.

3. *Conversation:* Talk about jargon! How did good things, like "telling the truth," "reasoned argument," "open-minded listening," "honest disagreement," and "warmly shared enthusiasm" ever get swallowed up by the cold term "communication"? Frequent, forthright, and humane conversation is the lifeblood of school reform.

4. *Collaboration:* Schools are bastions of isolation. Teachers often work separated from colleagues and parents; students often feel alone in a crowded classroom; principals are often rarely seen. All of these groups must feel like colleagues in the effort to change the school.

5. *Caring:* What a school is depends more on how people treat each other than on anything else. There is no slogan, no software, no shortcut to this most basic of values. That old adage "relationship first, task second" applies equally to a class or a committee.

6. *Conviviality:* It's all well and good to articulate a philosophy of school reform and pursue it in a concentrated and committed way. But somebody's got to buy the pizzas, bring in the birthday balloons, and spice up the meetings with fancy pastry and lousy jokes. Conviviality is a quality of acceptance, geniality, and good-naturedness. It's creating a culture where people are known and valued for who they are, not just for the work they do.[6]

No Excuses

When I was the principal at Shoreham-Wading River Middle School, another town in New York wanted to build a middle school modeled after ours. So they asked if they could send all kinds of people down to look at us. First, they sent the teachers down, and the teachers looked around and said, this is fantastic, but our administration will never go for it. Then the teachers left and the school board came down. The school board said, this is fantastic, but we don't think we could ever get our principals to do it. And then the principals came down and said (take a wild guess), this is great, but we could never get our teachers or our school board to do it.

This is a true story. I was the only one they were all coming to, so I was the only one who held all this information. Honestly, they had no idea that they were all copping out. They didn't think they were making excuses; they really thought that they were just being realistic about how things were. If I hadn't spoken up, nothing would have happened! Finally, I pulled everyone together and said, "Look, you guys all said you liked this and didn't think the others would, but they do, so what are you gonna do about it?" And that's how we got them on board. Change is possible. Most people really want things to be better.

When I was at Shoreham, I heard about a principal from another school who was saying about our innovative programs, "Oh, of course he can do that there, it's a rich school." Years later, when I was at Thayer, I heard that this same principal was saying, "Oh, of course he can do that at Thayer, it's a poor school." Incredible.

A lot of people call The Met an "alternative" school. The ones who think this is a bad thing assume that what we do is based on a bunch of wild, "out there" ideas that only apply to wild, "out there" kids. Even people who think "alternative schooling" is a good thing still see it as unnatural and full of risks. But to me, alternative schooling is like alternative medicine. What we in the United States call "alternative" medicine is based on ingredients that arise naturally from the earth, whereas "regular" medicine relies on artificial, synthetic ingredients.

The Met is actually based on some of the most mainstream ideas and widely accepted theories in numerous disciplines. Recent brain research shows that people learn by making sense of information, by producing knowledge, by connecting things, and by learning in a real context. Developmental psychology tells us that kids are fragile and need to be nurtured so that they can thrive. Gang research tells us that young people need to feel a part of a culture, part of something larger than themselves. Learning theory asserts the value of hands-on experiences. Mel Levine, famed pediatrician and best-selling author of *A Mind at a Time,* pleads with us to recognize that every child learns differently and that standardized tests and curricula hurt kids rather than help them. He calls for educators to "make a firm social and political commitment to neuro-developmental pluralism."[7]

These are not wild ideas; they are the *right* ideas. And **there is no excuse for not doing the right thing to improve kids' lives.** Rich, poor, middle-class, urban, rural, suburban—anyone connected in any way to a school district can help get this change started. You have no idea what you can do until you go do it.

Make It Happen

When should change happen? The great humanitarian Albert Schweitzer put it this way: "Truth has no special time of its own. Its hour is now, always, and indeed then most truly when it seems most unsuitable to actual circumstances."[8] Martin Luther King Jr. said, "The time is always right to do what is right."

So . . . the time is **NOW, NOW, NOW!**

If you are a parent or a teacher or a principal or an administrator or a politician or even a kid, start right now by creating your own vision of how your school might become a great school. Start this as an internal dialogue, use the margins of this book or a journal to sketch out your first ideas, and then get together with people around you and begin to build a collective vision. **Imagine what your school would look like if the changes you imagine began to take hold.** Live off that beauty and let it push you on.

Yes, we were lucky when we started The Met because we got to start from scratch. Our only real constraint was, "What's best for kids?" I know that most of you reading this book haven't had that opportunity, but that's OK: You can still think like we did. You're reading this book. **If you've gotten this far, you must at least care about kids and education, and that's a start.** And none of us is really starting from scratch if we remember and learn from our history. From John Dewey to Ted Sizer, many people and institutions have contributed bricks to the foundation of the kind of education reform that is possible today and in the future. So please **don't let excuses stop you from dreaming, or stop you from doing something (even just one thing) to change your school or the schools in your community for the better.**

And don't let wrong-minded policies or systems get in your way, either. Someone once said to me, "School bureaucracies do not change because they see the light, but because they feel the heat." A study I read about recently found that the one thing the greatest managers in the world have in common is that they do not hesitate to **break the rules.**[9] I believe that special leaders figure out how to work around faulty systems and take rule breaking a step further, so that broken rules become accepted rules. If you start by doing something that works, people take notice and want to do the same thing in other places. This is how bad rules get broken and replaced by better policies. It happens on a small scale and on the largest scale, in the small picture and in the big picture.

There are tons of examples out there. The trend over the past 50 years has been to build large schools, especially in urban areas. Then some educators started breaking the rules. They put four small schools in one large building. Then they demanded that autonomous small schools be built. Soon state legislators took on the charge. In the end, the U.S. Department of Education allocated millions of dollars to break large schools up into small schools.

I know of a high school where an English teacher decided to break the rules and have her kids develop portfolios and do exhibitions in place of tests. The whole department decided to follow suit, and then the social studies teachers did it, too. Pretty soon, the whole school had moved to portfolios and exhibitions as assessment tools. The superintendent was impressed with the results, so he set up a districtwide plan to phase in a policy of graduation by portfolio and exhibition.

No matter who you are or what role you play in the local school or education system, you can effect change. Here are some ideas to get you started.

If you are a parent:

* Join the school board, or at least go to school board meetings.
* Fight for the right to send your kid to the public school that meets his or her needs.
* Invite your kid's friends over and hold an informal dinner table discussion about how they think their school could be made better. (Make sure to have pizza.)

If you are a student:

* Ask a teacher to do a course on education reform.
* Demand that the student council be included in making real decisions about the school.
* Work with the faculty to develop a student evaluation process for each class.

If you are a teacher:

∗ Start a reading group around this book, or any book that would stimulate conversation about what schools should be.

∗ Ask your students to evaluate your classes, and ask your colleagues to do the same; use the information to improve teaching and learning in your school.

∗ Have dinner at your students' homes.

∗ Have your class (or classes) design their perfect school and compare it to their present school.

∗ Have your students interview someone who works in their field of interest to discover what skills they'll need to become what they want to be.

∗ Don't stop at any of these actions. Keep going, keep learning, keep climbing out of the box.

If you are a principal:

∗ Encourage your parents, students, and teachers to do everything on these lists, and much, much more.

∗ Recognize that you are accountable to your students far beyond their graduation from your school. If your goal is to create successful, lifelong learners, then your accountability to your students must follow them into their adult lives and careers.

If you are a college president, admissions officer, or administrator:

∗ See this book as a call to arms for you, as well. Figure out what you need to do so that high schools can stop focusing on preparing kids for college and start preparing them for life.

∗ Recognize how people learn best and how adults approach learning, and stop relying so much on textbooks and lecture halls—especially in students' first and second years of college.

∗ Make your classes smaller. Even in a small college, many of the introductory courses have hundreds of students. Now that we finally understand that 30 or 40 kids is too many in a high school classroom, we must acknowledge that college students would benefit from smaller classes, too.

* Start valuing the students' progress over their four years of high school as much as you value where they are when they graduate.
* Start figuring out ways to translate the work that small, innovative schools are doing into more inclusive admission requirements. Understand that the current practice of relying more heavily on the SAT/ACT scores of students who have learned in nontraditional environments is completely backward.
* Make sure your admission policies reflect the research that shows the bias of standardized tests against poor and minority students.
* Look at, and act on, the difference between college *acceptance* rates and college *completion* rates of poor and minority students.
* Understand, and act on, the fact that colleges are the gatekeepers of social mobility and that too many of our young people come to you with the cards already stacked against them.

Finally, if you are simply a community member:

* Join the local school board, or show up at school board meetings and add your voice to the discussion.
* Mentor a student.
* Find out what needs to be done at one of your local schools and see how you might help through donations of time or resources.
* Start a youth mentorship program at your workplace.
* Set up a discussion group about this book with colleagues or friends.

I believe that the philosophy of education that we've put into practice at The Met and in Big Picture Schools is right. Schools should be educating and evaluating one student at a time, using real work and the standards of the real world. Schools should be allowing kids to follow their interests and should be connecting them to adults and the outside world. Schools should be engaging every family in their child's learning and the life of the school. The specifics—*how* we do it at The Met, and how we encourage others to do it—is what we will keep looking at and what we must never be afraid to change.

So I ask you: What's it going to be? If you're an educator, does the enormity of the task make retreating to your classroom or office to tinker with testing schedules and pep rallies seem like a much safer idea? Or does it make your blood boil that our professional lives and the futures of our students are held hostage to school structures, climates, and curricula that fall far short of what they might be? Even given the perpetually underfunded condition of education, huge changes *are* possible and necessary—and it's the responsibility of both professional educators and everyday people to accept the challenge of seeing them through. Education *is* everyone's business. **You may now begin changing the world.**

Questions to Further This Conversation . . .

1. How can you foster the ability of the students or people around you to think "outside of the box"?

2. The Met and Big Picture Schools hold themselves accountable to the mantras of "one student at a time," "real work," "learning through interests," and "family engagement." What are the mantras you hold yourself accountable to?

3. Think of a current problem or challenge in your school, workplace, or personal life. How could you view this problem as "a friend"? How could you view it as an opportunity for change or a way to do something differently?

4. What is your vision for your school, your workplace, your family, or your personal life? How are you going to make it happen? What resources, mentors, or other sources of support will you use? What will keep you on the path toward your vision?

5. What are *you* going to do to change the world?

Notes

Foreword

1. Lipsitz, Joan. *Successful Schools for Young Adolescents.* New Brunswick, NJ: Transaction Books, 1984.
2. Krasner, Leonard. *Environmental Design and Human Behavior.* New York: Pergamon, 1980, p. 173.
3. Kammeraad-Campbell, Susan. *Doc: The Story of Dennis Littky and His Fight for a Better School.* Chicago: Contemporary Books, 1989.

Preface

1. Myles Horton (1905–1990) believed passionately in people's power to change the world. Inspired by the progressive education philosophy of John Dewey and the Danish folk school movement of the 1800s, in 1932, Horton founded the Highlander Folk School in Monteagle, Tennessee. Under Horton's leadership, the school was involved in union organizing during the 1930s and 1940s and in the civil rights movement in the 1950s and 1960s. The Highlander Research and Education Center remains active today. According to the organization's Web site, "Highlander's work is rooted in the belief that in a truly just and democratic society, the policies shaping political and economic life must be informed by equal concern for and participation by all people. Guided by this belief, we help communities that suffer from unfair government policies and big-business practices as they voice their concerns and join with others to form movements for change." Read more at http://www.highlandercenter.org.
2. Tom Peters's best-selling books on business include *A Passion for Excellence* (1984, with Nancy Austin), *Thriving on Chaos* (1987), and *Liberation Management* (1992). In 1999, National Public Radio named Tom's *In Search of Excellence* (1982, with Robert J. Waterman Jr.) as one of the "Top Three Business Books of the Century." *Fortune* calls Tom "the Ur-guru of management" To read more about Tom, go to http://www.tompeters.com.

3. Levine, Eliot. *One Kid at a Time: Big Lessons from a Small School.* New York: Teachers College Press, 2002.

Chapter 1

1. For more on "emotional IQ," see Goleman, Daniel. *Emotional Intelligence: Why It Can Matter More Than IQ.* New York: Bantam Books, 1995.
2. Boyer, Ernest L. "Making the Connections." This speech was delivered March 27, 1993, at the Annual Conference of the Association for Supervision and Curriculum Development in Washington, DC.
3. Exhibitions are public presentations of a student's learning. At The Met, exhibitions are a main method of assessment. Each student gives a quarterly exhibition on their learning, progress, and gaps, and answers questions and receives feedback from their panel. Each panel consists of the student's family members, advisor, and internship mentor, along with peers, other staff, and invited community members. For more on exhibitions, see Chapter 8.
4. Schneps, Matthew H., and Philip M. Sadler (Producers). *A Private Universe* [Videotape]. Harvard-Smithsonian Center for Astrophysics, 1987. For ordering information, call 1-800-LEARNER or visit http://www.learner.org.
5. Magliozzi, Tom, and Ray Magliozzi. *In Our Humble Opinion: Car Talk's Click and Clack Rant and Rave.* New York: Berkeley Publishing Group, 2000, p. 247.
6. Sternberg, Robert J. "What Is 'Successful' Intelligence?" *Education Week 16,* no. 11 (13 November 1996): 37.
7. Langer, Ellen. *Mindfulness.* Reading, MA: Addison-Wesley, 1989.
8. Langer, Ellen. *The Power of Mindful Learning.* Reading, MA: Addison-Wesley, 1997.
9. Ellen Langer, quoted in "Are You Living Mindlessly" by Michael Ryan. *Parade* (1 March 1998): 8.
10. Joseph Hart (1876–1949) was a progressive educator and social reformer and the author of *Light from the North: The Danish Folk Highschools, Their Meaning for America* (1927). He was an important influence on Myles Horton.

Chapter 2

1. Greene, Jay P., and Greg Forster. *Public High School Graduation and College Readiness Rates in the United States* [Education Working Paper, no. 3]. New York: Manhattan Institute for Policy Research, September 2003. Available: http://www.manhattan-institute.org/html/ewp_03.htm. During personal communication with Greg Forster (17 February 2004), he explained that this study relied on enrollment data, which are consistent from state to state, rather than dropout counts, which vary widely in validity from state to state. According to Forster, most dropout studies are unreliable due to the myriad definitions of what qualifies as "a dropout." For example, some states do not count as dropouts those students who dropped out of school but later went on to get a GED. Greene and Forster believe that counting GED recipients as having completed high school is misleading if the purpose of the study is to measure the success of the traditional high school system.

2. Centers for Disease Control and Prevention. "Web-based Injury Statistics Query and Reporting System (WISQARS)" [Web site]. Available: http://www.cdc.gov/ncipc/wisqars [27 March 2003].

3. Maguire, Kathleen, and Ann L. Pastore (Eds.). *Sourcebook of Criminal Justice Statistics* (30th ed.), pp. 352–353. Available: http://www.albany.edu/sourcebook/ [9 February 2004].

4. De Pree, Max. *Leading Without Power: Finding Hope in Serving Community.* San Francisco: Jossey-Bass, 1997, p. 151.

5. Altenbaugh, R. J. (Ed.). *Historical Dictionary of American Education.* Westport, CT: Greenwood Press, 1999, p. 90.

6. Ibid.

7. Dewey, John. *Experience and Education* (1938). New York: Touchstone, 1997.

8. Boyer, Ernest L. "Making the Connections."

9. Oliver Goldsmith (1728–1774) was an Irish playwright best known for *The Vicar of Wakefield* (1766) and *She Stoops to Conquer* (1773).

10. Reich, Robert B. "One Education Does Not Fit All." *The New York Times* (11 July 2000): A25, col. 2. Also available at *The American Prospect Online*: http://www.prospect.org/webfeatures/2000/07/reich-r-07-11.html.

11. Fried, Robert L. *The Passionate Teacher: A Practical Guide.* Boston: Beacon Press, 1995.

12. Fried, Robert L. *The Passionate Learner: How Teachers and Parents Can Help Children Reclaim the Joy of Discovery.* Boston: Beacon Press, 2001.

13. Littky, Dennis, and Robby Fried. "The Challenge to Make Good Schools Great." *NEA Today 6,* no. 6 (January 1988): 4–8.

14. National Commission on Excellence on Education. "A Nation at Risk: The Imperative of Educational Reform." Washington, DC: Author (April 1983). Available: http://www.ed.gov/pubs/NatAtRisk/index.html.

15. This survey, featuring questions designed to gauge students', teachers', and parents' attitudes about and experiences in school, is conducted annually as part of the "self-study" activities required under the Rhode Island Department of Education's School Accountability for Learning and Teaching (SALT) program. The statistics cited here are from the "2003 Selected School Climate Students' Report of Usage and Helpfulness of School Services [ST-H-C.5]." Current and archived "SALT survey" results data from The Met and other Rhode Island schools are available online from the Rhode Island Department of Education: http://www.ridoe.net or http://www.infoworks.ride.uri.edu/2004/reports/salt.asp.

Chapter 3
1. Krasner, Leonard. *Environmental Design and Human Behavior,* p. 173.

2. Lipsitz, Joan. *Successful Schools for Young Adolescents,* p. 168.

3. Wood, George. *Schools That Work: America's Most Innovative Public Education Programs.* New York: Plume, Penguin Books, 1992, p. 112.

4. Katherine Graham (1917–2003) was owner and publisher of *The Washington Post.*

5. See "2002–2003 Parent Attitudes Towards the School and Involvement [PA-A.2]" in the State of Rhode Island 2003 SALT Survey Reports. Available: http://www.infoworks.ride.uri.edu/2002/reports/salt.asp.

6. Dewey, John. *Experience and Education*, p. 63.

7. Ibid., p. 62.

8. Deborah Meier. Personal communication, 19 May 1998.

9. My partner Elliot Washor has passionately studied how to make form follow function when designing school facilities. You can read an abridged version of his dissertation on the topic, titled "Innovative Pedagogy and School Facilities," at http://www.designshare.com/research/washor/InnovativePedagogyAndFacilities.asp.

10. De Pree, Max. *Leading Without Power,* p. 24.

11. Wood, op. cit., p. 55.

12. Lipsitz, op. cit., pp. 132–133.

13. For a great review of research about small schools, see Michael Klonsky's *Small Schools: The Numbers Tell a Story.* Small Schools Workshop, The University of Illinois at Chicago Publications Series, 1995 (ordering information and additional resources are available at http://www.smallschoolsworkshop.org) and "Small Schools, Big Results" [online] from the KnowledgeWorks Foundation: http://www.kwfdn.org. Another essential resource is "School Size, School Climate, and Student Performance," Kathleen Cotton's report for the Northwest Regional Educational Laboratory, which surveys all the major research between 1981 and 1996 on the relationship between school size and school quality. It's available at http://www.nwrel.org/scpd/sirs/10/c020.html.

14. "CPS Targets Gun Violence" [Press release]. Chicago: Chicago Public Schools, 24 January 2004. Available: http://www.cps.k12.il.us/AboutCPS/PressReleases/January_2004/gun_violence.htm.

15. Toch, Thomas. "Small Schools, Big Ideas." *Education Week 23,* no. 14 (3 December 2003): 44.

16. Conant, James B. *The American High School Today: A First Report to Interested Citizens.* New York: McGraw-Hill, 1959.

17. Toch, op. cit., p. 44.

Chapter 4

1. Zander, Rosamund Stone, and Benjamin Zander. *The Art of Possibility.* Boston: Harvard Business School Press, 2000, p. 26.

2. John Ciardi (1916–1986) was a poet, writer, and teacher.

3. The Center for Education Reform. "The Textbook Conundrum." Washington, DC: Author (May 2001): 1. Available: http://www.edreform.com/_upload/textbook.pdf or by writing to The Center for Education Reform, Suite 204, 1001 Connecticut Avenue, NW, Washington, DC 20036.

4. Dewey, John. *Experience and Education,* p. 57.

5. Dewey said it this way: "I am not romantic enough about the young to suppose that every pupil will respond or that any child of normally strong impulses will respond on every occasion. There are likely to be some who, when they come to school, are already victims of injurious conditions outside of the school and who have become so passive and unduly docile that they fail to contribute. There will be others who, because of previous experience, are bumptious and unruly and perhaps downright rebellious. But it is certain that the general principle of social control cannot be predicated upon such cases. It is also true that no

general rule can be laid down for dealing with such cases. The teacher has to deal with them individually. They fall into general classes, but no two are exactly alike. The educator has to discover as best he or she can the causes for the recalcitrant attitudes." (*Experience and Education,* p. 56)

Chapter 5

1. "Information Works! Measuring Rhode Island's Schools for Change: State Report Card." Providence, RI: Rhode Island Department of Education, 2003, p. 38. Available: http://www.infoworks.ride.uri.edu/2003/state.
2. Steinberg, Adria. "Forty-Three Valedictorians: Graduates of The Met Talk About Their Learning." *Jobs for the Future* [online]: 22. Available: http://www.jff.org/jff/kc/library/0053.
3. John Holt (1923–1985) was an outspoken advocate for education reform, children's rights, and alternative schooling. He authored several books, including *How Children Learn* (1964/1995).
4. This story, told by William (Bill) Severns, president of the Performing Arts Center of Los Angeles County, was reprinted in "Do It," Stony Brook Teacher Training Complex Newsletter (Fall 1971): 4.
5. Sternberg, Robert J. "What Is 'Successful' Intelligence?" p. 48.
6. Denis Diderot (1713–1784) was a French Enlightenment philosopher.
7. Beem, Edgar Allen. "Mama Mia!" *Teacher Magazine 14,* no. 3 (November/December 2002): 14.
8. Ibid., p. 13.
9. Csikszentmihalyi, Mihaly, and Barbara Schneider. *Becoming Adult: How Teenagers Prepare for the World of Work.* New York: Basic Books, 2000.
10. Ibid., p. 19.

Chapter 6

1. Wolk, Ron. "Bored of Education." *Teacher Magazine 13,* no. 3 (November/December 2001): 3.
2. Thich Nhat Hanh is a Vietnamese Buddhist monk and peace activist.
3. Csikszentmihalyi, Mihaly, and Barbara Schneider. *Becoming Adult,* p. 18.
4. Miller, George A. "The Magical Number Seven, Plus or Minus Two: Some Limits on Our Capacity for Processing Information." *The Psychological Review 63* (1956): 81–97.
5. Steinberg, Adria. "Forty-Three Valedictorians," p. 5.
6. *The Met Implementation Plan*, 1995, p. 11. Additional information on The Met's philosophy and practices is available at http://www.bigpicture.org.
7. Illich, Ivan. *Deschooling Society.* London: Marion Boyars Publishers Ltd., 1996, p. 73.
8. *The Met Implementation Plan*, p. 16.
9. Howard A. Adams is director of the GEM National Institute on Mentoring at the Georgia Institute of Technology.
10. Al Capp (1909–1979) was a cartoonist and the creator of *L'il Abner.*

Chapter 7

1. Lipsitz, Joan. *Successful Schools for Young Adolescents,* p. 155.

Chapter 8

1. Thomas Huxley (1825–1895) was a British zoologist and philosopher best known for his advocacy and defense of Darwinism. He wrote and spoke about numerous related topics, including social issues and education.

2. Kohn, Alfie. "From Degrading to De-Grading." *High School Magazine 6,* no. 5 (March 1999): 38–43. Available: http://www.alfiekohn.org/teaching/fdtd-g.htm.

3. For additional information, see "Transition from Middle School into High School," by Nancy B. Mizelle and Judith L. Irvin, published in the May 2000 issue of *Middle School Journal.* The article is available online at http://www.nmsa.org/research/res_articles_may2000.htm.

4. Thomas, Karen. "Colleges Clamp Down on Cheaters." *USA Today* (11 June 2001): 3D. Available: http://www.usatoday.com/life/2001-06-11-cheaters.htm.

5. Steinberg, Adria. "Forty-Three Valedictorians," p. 8.

6. Dewey, John. *The School and Society* (1915). Carbondale: Southern Illinois University Press, 1980, pp. 66–67.

Chapter 8½

1. Wesson, Kenneth. "The Volvo Effect." *Education Week 20,* no. 12 (22 November 2000): 34.

2. Reich, Robert B. "One Education Does Not Fit All," A25, col. 2.

3. Ibid.

4. Sternberg, Robert J. "What Is 'Successful' Intelligence?" p. 48.

5. "Let Them Eat Tests." *FairTest Examiner 15,* no. 1, (Winter 2000–2001): 1. Available: http://www.fairtest.org/nattest/Bush%20ExamWinter01.html.

6. Popham, W. James. *The Truth About Testing: An Educator's Call to Action.* Alexandria, VA: Association for Supervision and Curriculum Development, 2001, pp. 40–41.

7. Ibid., p. 43.

8. Ibid., p. 74.

Chapter 9

1. Horton, Myles, with Judith Kohl and Herbert Kohl. *The Long Haul: An Autobiography.* New York: Doubleday, 1990, p. 131.

2. Ibid., pp. 107–108.

3. Walker, D. F. *Fundamentals of Curriculum: Passion and Professionalism* (2nd ed.). Mahwah, NJ: Lawrence Erlbaum Associates, 2003, p. 5.

4. Littky, Dennis. "Moving Towards a Vision." In Edward R. Ducharme and Douglas S. Fleming (Eds.), *The Rural and Small School Principalship: Practice, Research, and Vision.* Chelmsford,

MA: Northeast Regional Exchange, Inc.; Washington, DC: National Institute of Education, U.S. Department of Education, 1985, p. 155.

5. Peters, Tom. *Thriving on Chaos.* New York: Knopf, 1987.

6. Littky, Dennis, and Robby Fried. "The Challenge to Make Good Schools Great," pp. 7–8.

7. Levine, Mel. *A Mind at a Time.* New York: Simon & Schuster, 2002, p. 335.

8. Cousins, Norman (Ed.). *The Words of Albert Schweitzer.* New York: Newmarket Press, 1996.

9. Buckingham, Marcus, and Curt Coffman. *First, Break all the Rules: What the World's Greatest Managers Do Differently.* New York: Simon & Schuster, 1999.

From Dennis's Bookshelf

I love reading: education books, magazines, novels, management books, memoirs, newspapers, everything. I read because I want to know everything. I want to know everything that went on and everything that's going on, so that I don't waste time trying to recreate what's already been done.

Earlier in my career, I was especially interested in reading books that confirmed what I believed. I liked hearing "my ideas" in other authors' voices—often, voices very different from mine—and I liked seeing valid research that backed these ideas up. Now, I like to read books that challenge me and help me to see the connections between the work of educators and everything else that is going on in the world. For example, management books are fun and help me get the strength to do my work as a leader. Life stories and social issues books are fascinating because they help me think about how social change relates to what we do in schools. I also love books of quotations because they give me a quick way of looking at what I'm doing from different perspectives, taking me further outside the education box.

Read the books and writers I mention throughout this book, and then read some from the following list. Read stuff that confirms your beliefs, but also read stuff that challenges your thinking. Read in the way that we want kids to read: to compare ideas, to see connections, to find meaning, to relate ideas and stories to our own lives, and to form opinions. And then read some more.

Albom, Mitch. (1997). *Tuesdays with Morrie: An Old Man, a Young Man, and Life's Greatest Lesson.* **New York: Doubleday.**
This is about one man's attitude toward life, and reading it made me think about what's really important in a school, what's really important for kids to learn, and who kids should be learning it from.

Alinsky, Saul. (1971). *Rules for Radicals: A Practical Primer for Realistic Radicals.* **New York: Vintage Books.**
This book reminds us how to make change in the world. Alinsky helped me think about organizing, whether it's organizing my students' parents, my teachers, or the kids themselves. In education, we are all community organizers.

Ayers, William, Michael Klonsky, and Gabrielle Lyon (Eds.). (2000). *A Simple Justice: The Challenge of Small Schools.* **New York: Teachers College Press.**
This is a book that looks at education through the lens of social justice. It contains lots of good, short articles by many of the people who've been fighting for social justice for a long time.

Banyai, Istvan. (1995). *Zoom.* **New York: Penguin Books USA, Inc.**
I don't even know what kind of book you'd call this. It's a picture book, but it helps you think about the smaller and bigger pictures, and about how the way we see things depends on the way we look at them. Every page shows a photo that zooms out further and further from the original, so you keep going "whoa!" as you get closer and closer to understanding the bigger picture. It reminds you that while you're working "up close" (like in a classroom or with your own child), you are also dealing with bigger issues like economics, social justice, and so on. Your work is so much broader than you think.

Barth, Roland S. (1990). *Improving Schools from Within: Teachers, Parents, and Principals Can Make the Difference.* **San Francisco: Jossey-Bass.**
This book talks in the most regular language about how to change schools. It's a great one. And Barth has continued to write great ones.

Coles, Robert. (1997). *The Moral Intelligence of Children.* **New York: Random House, Inc.**
Coles has always had this sophisticated but simple way of looking at and talking about kids and greatly respecting them. In this book, he helps us focus on who kids are.

Cousins, Norman. (1960). *Dr. Schweitzer of Lambaréné.* **New York: Harper & Brothers.**

Albert Schweitzer did all this great work setting up a hospital in Africa and completely committed himself to making change in the world, yet he took all kinds of criticism. This book has helped me as a leader by helping me understand that not everyone is going to like you. It has helped me to be stronger and bolder.

Cousins, Norman. (1981). *Human Options: An Autobiographical Notebook.* **New York: W. W. Norton & Company.**

This is Cousins's autobiography, told through his experiences with the many famous people he met while working as the editor of the *Saturday Review.* I loved this book because of the way it highlights the importance of human connections.

Csikszentmihalyi, Mihaly. (1990). *Flow: The Psychology of Optimal Experience.* **New York: Harper & Row.**

This is about what we try to get our kids into at The Met: "the flow." It's about getting in the zone—having a great day when you become one with what you're working on. It's about engaging kids in their learning.

Csikszentmihalyi, Mihaly, and Barbara Schneider. (2000). *Becoming Adult: How Teenagers Prepare for the World of Work.* **New York: Basic Books.**

This is a book by a great researcher whose findings support the work we're doing at The Met and in our Big Picture Schools. The ideas about depth as opposed to breadth and how learning something very deeply makes people good thinkers are especially relevant.

Cullum, Albert. (1971). *The Geranium on the Window Sill Just Died, but Teacher You Went Right On.* **New York: Harlin Quist, Inc.**

This short picture/poetry book makes the point about what teaching really means better than most academic texts I have read. In the most simple way, it shows what the truth is—for kids, for teachers, and for the system as a whole.

De Pree, Max. (1987). *Leadership Is an Art.* **East Lansing, MI: Michigan State University Press.**
This is one of my favorite books. I used it as my text once when I was tutoring a man who'd never learned how to read—a young guy who was about to take over his dad's company. And then I got hooked on Max De Pree and everything he had to say about leadership. The beautiful words of this book confirm to me that I'm doing the right thing. We are all leaders, so De Pree's books are really for all of us. Another of my favorites is his *Leadership Jazz* (1992), which talks about leadership as not just something you do on a job, but as a total way of being and living in the world.

Evans, Nicholas. (1995). *The Horse Whisperer.* **New York: Delacorte Press.**
This book about a horse trainer with unusual methods makes me think a lot about the usual methods of working with kids and how we might do things differently. The guy in the book believes in literally *talking* to horses, in really trying to understand each individual horse. And even though he is very successful and can take wild horses and train them without whipping them or doing any of the usual things, everyone thinks he is full of it. Then he is anointed by the Queen, and this becomes the "tipping point" for him (see Gladwell, next). It makes me wonder who will "anoint us" in our work to be more humane toward kids.

Gladwell, Malcolm. (2000). *The Tipping Point: How Little Things Can Make a Big Difference.* **Boston: Little, Brown and Company.**
This book made me think about how social changes come about, and how, as the subtitle says, little things really *can* make a big difference. For example, Gladwell talks about how a fashion designer's vacation in Maine led to Hush Puppies shoes (manufactured in Maine for years and worn by a relatively small number of people) becoming a footwear sensation, with annual sales in the hundreds of thousands. What are the tipping points that will change the way we do education?

Holt, John. (1967). *How Children Learn.* **New York: Pitman Publishing.**
This book was very important to me back in the late '60s. Holt was one of those strong critics of education who believed in educating one child at a time. Reading him before I even knew how strongly I agreed with him was

very important. There are lots of parallels between his work and what I've written in this book, nearly 40 years later.

Illich, Ivan. (1971). *Deschooling Society.* **New York: Harper & Row.**
The title alone is a challenging concept: How could schooling work without school buildings? This book challenges you to reexamine everything you have ever thought you understood about the traditional education system.

Karsh, Yousuf. (1983). *Karsh: A Fifty-Year Retrospective.* **Boston: Little, Brown and Company.**
This book helped me understand what a brilliant photograph looks like and how people and their stories look different when you look at them differently. Karsh was primarily a portrait photographer, and here he shows famous people in ways you've never seen them before. I also love the little stories he tells next to each photo, which take you even deeper into these people we think we understand so well.

Kinsella, W. P. (1982). *Shoeless Joe.* **Boston: Houghton-Mifflin.**
During a conversation I had with the head of a foundation about getting some money for my work, she told me that before she would talk to me any further, I had to go out and read this book. So I did, and it was one of those books I just didn't want to end. I read the last pages so slowly, savoring them. It's about believing in miracles, about how anything is possible. And it's better than the movie version (*Field of Dreams*) that followed.

Kohl, Herbert R. (1969). *The Open Classroom: A Practical Guide to a New Way of Teaching.* **New York: New York Review.**
This book was an eye-opener, presenting a different kind of education. It really influenced my thinking as I started my first school, Shoreham-Wading River Middle School.

Kohl, Herbert R. (1998). *The Discipline of Hope: Learning from a Lifetime of Teaching.* **New York: Simon & Schuster.**
Herb, now a friend, is a deep thinker who thinks about more than just education. He thinks about race, politics, and economics and continues to write good, straightforward books that support kids.

Kosinski, Jerzy. (1970). *Being There.* **New York: Harcourt Brace Jovanovich.**
This is a book about the simplicity of things. How simple life really is. How you only see what you want to see.

Kozol, Jonathan. (1991). *Savage Inequalities: Children in America's Schools.* **New York: Crown Publishers.**
Most of my passion for change comes from anger. This book helped me get angrier.

Levine, Eliot. (2002). *One Kid at a Time: Big Lessons from a Small School.* **New York: Teachers College Press.**
Anyone reading this book has to read Eliot's book on The Met. He spent two years really studying exactly how we do what we do. Here, he tells it like it was, with no sugarcoating. After finishing the book, Eliot chose to immerse himself even more; he became an advisor at The Met.

McPhee, John. (1966). *Headmaster: Frank L. Boyden, of Deerfield.* **New York: Farrar, Straus & Giroux.**
This is the story of a man who signed on for what he thought would be a one-year job teaching English at Deerfield Academy in Massachusetts. Sixty-six years later he retired as the headmaster. Boyden's desk was in the middle of the school hallway, and no one could get in or out of the school without talking to him. This book is a beautiful portrait of someone who is passionate about education.

Peters, Thomas J., and Robert H. Waterman Jr. (1982). *In Search of Excellence: Lessons from America's Best-Run Companies.* **New York: Warner Books.**
I was a young school leader riding on a ferryboat from Long Island to Connecticut when I first read Tom Peters's and Bob Waterman's eight principles for great companies and realized they were the same ideas I was using in my work. People had been telling me that my approach was "soft"; this book helped me see that what I was doing were the kinds of things that make companies great. For example, for an hour of our staff retreat one year, I had our

music teacher bring us together to play as a group. My superintendent couldn't believe he was paying us for that. But in this book, the authors tell a similar story of a company renting a football field and playing games together, and they present it as this big, important strategy for making a great company.

Postman, Neil, and Charles Weingartner. (1969). *Teaching as a Subversive Activity.* **New York: Delacorte Press.**
This is a kick-in-the-butt book about doing things differently. Even the title shakes up the traditional ways of talking about teaching.

Rand, Ayn. (1943). *The Fountainhead.* **Indianapolis, IN: Bobbs-Merrill.**
As a kid, I was not much of a reader. I remember this as one of the first books I couldn't put down. The main character is a man who refuses to compromise: a purist. Although he is constantly losing according to the standards of the world around him, in reality, through his pureness, he is winning. I've read this book many times over the years, and it continues to inspire me to do what is right and to refuse to compromise on what I believe is best for kids.

Sarason, Seymour. (1971). *The Culture of the School and the Problem of Change.* **Boston: Allyn & Bacon.**
This is a very significant book that looks at research and schools in a different way. Seymour is a great thinker; now in his eighties, he continues to put out about a book a year. Each is different and all are incredibly thoughtful. He has become a friend because in person, like in his books, he always asks good, tough questions.

Sizer, Theodore. (1984). *Horace's Compromise: The Dilemma of the American High School.* **Boston: Houghton Mifflin.**
This book caused a stir when it was published. Ted is a former Harvard dean, and in this book, he confirmed in a research-y way what lots of educators had been saying for years: that U.S. schools were not doing the job we needed them to do and we needed to try something different. Ted's nine common principles really gelled with me.

Wood, George H. (1992). *Schools That Work: America's Most Innovative Public Education Programs.* **New York: Plume, Penguin Books.**
This is a book by a guy who got so excited about the four schools he had written about that he left his college teaching job to become a principal. Of course, I particularly like this book because it profiles one of my schools, but it's also a nice, straightforward description of good schools.

Zander, Rosamund Stone, and Benjamin Zander. (2000). *The Art of Possibility.* **Boston: Harvard Business School Press.**
What's great about this book is it is full of possibilities. It's about becoming who you want to be, creating your own reality, believing in things. It's a book I've used a lot to help people believe that they can create the environment they want to live in, learn in, and educate in.

Acknowledgments

For a long time, I have been looking for a way to tell the stories of my schools in a way that would inspire people to think differently and take action. I'll begin this section with an overall thanks to the friends and colleagues who have been urging me to write a book for as long as I can remember. Some of them read early drafts or contributed to the book in other ways, and I am grateful to them for their support (especially Seymour, Roland, Debbie, Seth, Danny, Wayne, Joe, Charly, Katie at ASCD, and everyone whose photo appears on the cover). Then I want to thank my assistant, Sam. She was the catalyst for this book, and I owe her many thanks. In fact, the process of writing this book is a great model for practitioners who want to write about their practice, stories, and ideas, but don't want to stop practicing to do so. To them, I say find a Sam Grabelle.

This book is about the philosophy behind the practice of education and so, for that, I am grateful for people like John Dewey and Ted Sizer, who set the groundwork for a drastic rethinking of schooling. Although I'm old, I never did get the chance to meet Dewey. But I first met Ted Sizer in the early '80s at a speech he was giving when I was beginning my tenure as a principal at Thayer Junior/Senior High School in Winchester, New Hampshire. There was this former dean of Harvard—a brilliant, seemingly traditional man— saying incredibly radical stuff about what was wrong with schools and what drastic steps we needed to take to change things. They were things I felt I was already doing at Thayer. When he finished his talk, I ran up to the front of the room, introduced myself, and just blurted out, "You're talking about it, I'm doing it! Let's get together! This is fantastic!" Minutes later, I just ran. I ran outside on pure adrenaline and threw up in the parking lot.

After that memorable introduction, Ted visited Thayer and selected us as one of the first schools to be involved in the Coalition of Essential Schools. I knew then that he was a person whose voice would be heard and accepted in places where my voice would not. I remember that the first time we really talked, he told me that we were soul mates. We were, and we continue to be. And neither of us has ever stepped away from our commitment to make schools better places for learning.

Speaking of soul mates, Deborah Meier was the first fellow practitioner I really connected with. She is one of the deepest thinkers I know. You can't ask Debbie a simple question without getting a great, complicated answer. I have loved my relationship with her, talking about everything from wearing hats in the school to the importance of adults connecting with kids. Anytime she writes something, it should be read.

The three of us—Ted, Debbie, and I—continue to struggle in our own realms and to talk whenever we can. We continue to think together about how to change education to bring it around to what we think it should be. So we talk about what position we should be in to have the most influence, whether this is a good time or a bad time to bring about change in the world, or how someone could try to change the world a little bit to help it be more conducive to small schools. When we three come together, it is to step back and look at the big picture.

At The Met, we ask every one of our kids to write a 75-page autobiography before they graduate. It forces them to look at their lives and their influences, just as I am doing now. They always talk about their struggles and thank the people who helped them get through it all. When I look at *my* life, I am reminded of the people who believed in me.

First, I look at my dad, mom, and sisters, Nancy and Sandy. They are the people who have given me the ultimate unconditional love that has allowed me to always be myself and to continue to take risks. I come from a wonderful combination—my mom was the kind of person who took action and pushed for what she wanted and my dad was very laid back and could handle nearly anything that life threw at him. I know they were proud that I became someone who works incredibly hard at the things I care about, but never lets things get me so crazy that I forget to see the joy and the fun in life.

My sisters are two incredible women, both educators. They have always been proud and supportive of who I am and what I do. It is beautiful to me that their families—their husbands, Irv and Jim, and my nieces and nephews, Neil, Helane, Stephanie, Seth, and Ari—are just as loving and supportive of me. I am a lucky man.

Shelly Levine has been my best friend since 1972, when he was the principal of Shoreham-Wading River's elementary school and I was the principal of its middle school. Shelly, I remember the reggae dancing after a school board meeting and the 20-mile run in 90-degree heat as we prepared for one of our marathons. I am grateful for your support and total confidence in me. It is wonderful to know that I have a friend of more than 30 years who knows my life inside and out, and who has never not been there.

Old friends are the people you don't want to forget in something as important as an acknowledgments section. It is my old friends who have taught me about mutual respect and the strength it gives you as you go about life. Thank you Danny, Sandy, Richard, and Howard. And Marilyn, David, Fred, and Mark . . . I miss you.

Many years ago, when I started college at Ann Arbor, I had an advisor, John Hagen, who believed in me, so *I* began to believe in me. And the guy who accepted me into graduate school, Bill Morse—I just talked to him last week. To this day, his support helps keep me going. And Lenora, Liz, Steve, and Rhody McCoy, from my very first job working with African American parents in Ocean Hill-Brownsville, it was you who helped me see that I had something to offer.

Then there are the friends and mentors who are also well-known educators: Seymour Sarason, George Wood, and Roland Barth, who constantly question and push me, but have always been supportive of what I am trying to do. And management guru Tom Peters, whose wisdom and wild thinking always inspires me. And the Hollywood folks, too: Michael Tucker, Jill Eikenberry, and producer Lyle Poncher, who got excited about my work after reading *Doc* and decided to turn it into a movie. Those years we spent working on it together gave me strength. I am proud to count each of you among my friends.

Peter McWalters has used the power he has as commissioner of education in the state of Rhode Island to support our ideas, many of which were *his* ideas. Having someone with his power believing in us has made an incredible difference, both in our survival and in our belief in ourselves. I'm not even sure he realizes how much he helps us. Ron Wolk, founder of *Education Week* and *Teacher Magazine,* supports our work by being president of our Big Picture Board.

And, if you can believe this, I really want to thank the funders (not to make them feel good or to encourage them to like our work more, of course). But when you connect with a funder, it gives you more than just money. When The Wallace Foundation gave us one million dollars to do principal leadership training, it not only told the world that they supported us, but also told us that they believed in what we were doing. And that helped us grow. The Bill & Melinda Gates Foundation has probably helped us and our work more than anything. We knew we had good schools. We knew we were going to expand eventually. But when Tom Vander Ark came along, and, as we say in a whisper, *anointed* us, it said to us and to the world that what we were doing was important. And then, when Kyle Miller came back three years later and said, "We like what you've done; now give us even more schools"—well, that drove us even harder. Their belief in us keeps us believing in ourselves.

When I was at Thayer and my job was on the line, the ones who believed in me and kept me going were community people, like Winnie, Frank, Marian, Marcia, Cyndy, Cindy, and Brooks. They were teachers, like Stephanie, Karen, Don, Barb, Marlene, and Val, among so many others. And they were kids, whose support helped me get through all the yelling and the fighting. Another was Jill Homberg, who continues to fight the good fight by my side at The Met. And, of course, one was Dick McCarthy, the superintendent who helped me survive by convincing people of the value of our work, even when they wouldn't listen to me.

I wish I could name all the people at my schools and thank them here for the way they treat kids and the way they've treated me. I especially want to thank the great assistants I've had who've helped keep my head on straight and allowed me to work harder and better. Thank you Farrell, Elizabeth, Lani, Rachel, Sam, and Sarah. And my principals at The Met. When I have dinner with a young principal and he asks me how I would have handled a certain situation when I was his age, it moves me, because it's then that I see that I am helping influence the next generation of leaders. The only thing I feel I can really leave behind when I'm gone is the group of people who believe in this kind of education and will keep fighting for better schools that care about kids. Charlie, Jill, Danique, Chris, Amy, Wayne, Nancy, and Phil: It has been very cool to watch you grow into incredible leaders. You all inspire me.

When I was struggling along with the teachers who helped me start Shoreham-Wading River, the teachers who stuck with me when I was new at Thayer, and the people who helped us start The Big Picture Company and The Met, I learned how at the beginning of anything, it is always about the people. When you struggle together, you get closer than you do in any other kind of situation. I don't need to list all the people because I think I have made sure that they know who they are. They were the believers before there was anything to believe in. I am grateful that many of them are still a part of my life, and that almost everyone who helped us start The Met and Big Picture are still with us, growing right along with me. Zelayne, Rachel, Keith, Brian, John, Anita, Elaine, and all the local parents who fought for us: You know I mean you.

Stanley Goldstein, the founder of CVS Pharmacy, is a wonderful, smart man whose support of our work makes the business world look at us differently. Stan has been dear to me over these last 13 years, not only because he is always there for me as a friend, but because he is a true mentor. He has been a main player in our work in Rhode Island through his roles as chairman of The Met Board of Directors and as an active member of The Big Picture Board. He has never wavered in his commitment and trust.

Finally, there is the cofounder of The Met and The Big Picture Company, my dear friend Elliot Washor. My relationship with Elliot has been great. Our energies work well together. Every Sunday for the last 12 years, we have met at my house for three or four hours of brainstorming and planning. Together, we are a powerful duo, working tirelessly and always believing in each other and in our ability to make significant change. Everything with us is about the ideas and the actions. Thinking, thinking, thinking. And doing, doing, doing. Elliot could just as well have written this book himself; our ideas and our passions have grown together.

I thank everyone who has been brave enough to step forward and take a risk—to try new things—to feel good, feel bad, and feel good again. It is amazing work. Take a step back . . . talk about it to family and friends . . . listen to your words . . . see for yourself what amazing work you are doing. Right now, I can think of hundreds of Met kids, staff, and families I saw yesterday or will see tomorrow who make it all worthwhile. I have one more TGIF to quote, from August 16, 2002: "I am a lucky man to be surrounded by amazing people and incredible projects. I am exactly where I want to be in my work and my life." Yes. Always. I thank each and every one of you.

All of this comes back to the passage from Misty's letter that I quoted in the Preface, which asked me who or what it was that gave me the idea for The Met. I have tried, throughout this book and here, to answer her by saying that it was the people. The random people I've met, the teachers I've learned from, the authors whose books I've read, the family I grew up in, the kids and families who have let me into their lives, the staffs who have worked beside me, and the friends who've challenged and supported me. For all of you who have helped bring me to this place, I am saying thank you for "whispering The Met into my ear." And I am yelling right back.

Index

About the Authors

Dennis Littky is director and cofounder of the Metropolitan Regional Career and Technical Center ("The Met"), in Providence, Rhode Island, and codirector and cofounder of The Big Picture Company, a nonprofit education reform organization that creates and supports small, personalized, public high schools that work in tandem with their communities.

Nationally known for his more than 35 years of innovative leadership in middle and secondary education, Dennis and his work have been featured in *The New York Times, The Boston Globe, Newsweek, Fortune,* and numerous books and journals. He was the subject of the 1992 NBC-TV movie *A Town Torn Apart,* based on the book *Doc* by Susan Kammeraad-Campbell, which chronicled his 13-year tenure as the principal of Thayer Junior/Senior High School in Winchester, New Hampshire. He has been honored as New Hampshire's Principal of the Year and was runner-up for the National Principal of the Year. Dennis, who holds a double Ph.D. in education and psychology from the University of Michigan, has also served as a senior fellow at Brown University's Annenberg Institute. In 2002, he was awarded the McGraw-Hill Company's Harold W. McGraw Jr. Prize in Education.

Samantha Grabelle is Dennis Littky's assistant at The Big Picture Company and The Met. She earned a B.A. with honors in multicultural education from Brown University and a master's degree in social work with a concentration in community organizing from the University of Connecticut School of Social Work, where she was named the Connecticut National Association of Social Workers' Social Work Student of the Year.

Sam grew up in Tinton Falls, New Jersey, with her parents, two older sisters, and baby brother, who was the first child she ever really knew. It was when he was born and she was 4 years old that she first discovered her life's purpose: to help make the world a better place for children. She would like to thank the people who believed in her: her family, friends, and especially her first true mentor, Julius Newman, professor of community organizing at UConn School of Social Work. And she would like to thank the kids at The Met, and all of the hundreds of "other people's children" with whom she's worked over the years for letting her be herself and always inspiring her writing.

Dennis and Sam welcome your feedback, comments, and stories at TheBigPicture@bigpicture.org.

[handwritten notes:]

". They say Knowledge is power. We say the use of Knowledge is power" p8

. Learning is personal

p.14

p.38 Schools must help kids gain knowledge believe in themselves, believe in others + love learning